Editor
Stephanie Buehler, Psy.D.

Editorial Project Manager
Ina Massler Levin, M.A.

Editor-in-Chief
Sharon Coan, M.S. Ed.

Illustrator
Victoria Ponikvar-l

Cover Artist
Jessica Orlando

Art Coordinator
Denice Adorno

Creative Director
Elayne Roberts

Imaging
Alfred Lau

Product Manager
Phil Garcia

Publisher
Mary D. Smith, M.S. Ed.

Clark

MEETING WRITING STANDARDS

Narrative Writing

Grades 3–5

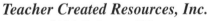

Written by

Andrea Trischitta, MA/MAT

Teacher Created Resources, Inc.
6421 Industry Way
Westminster, CA 92683
www.teachercreated.com

ISBN-1-57690-988-3

©2000 Teacher Created Resources, Inc.
Reprinted, 2005
Made in U.S.A.

Table of Contents

Introduction

Teaching narrative writing can be revitalizing. With a single assignment, the teacher receives narratives that reflect each student's personality and life. Thus, reading student narratives will always be different, no matter how many times the writing assignment is given.

Because narrative writing encompasses both nonfiction and fiction, writing teachers have the opportunity to allow students to explore not only themselves but also the lives of others. *Narrative Writing* guides students through the writing process, challenging and engaging writers at all levels to produce stories worth telling, sharing, and saving. In *Narrative Writing*, teachers will find thought-provoking narrative writing activities, ideas for publishing student work, and ways to use technology. Also included are lessons on the elements of narrative writing, figurative language, grammar, and proofreading/editing skills. Students can learn firsthand how to combine many essential skills to create a successful narrative. Teachers may work through the lessons, leading the students to writing, revising, and editing full narratives, but teachers should also feel free to adapt the lessons to meet the needs of their class. Whatever the decision, each activity will assist in the creation of a narrative, and the more practice students have in writing narratives, the better they are at writing them.

The graphic organizers included in *Narrative Writing* help students organize their thoughts, concentrate on a particular aspect of narrative writing, and provide an excellent visual tool that assists in writing narratives. Original narratives included in *Narrative Writing* will inspire the most recalcitrant writers, and provide springboards for analysis of style and technique, as well as discussion. There are also checklists for self-revision and reader-response, as well as rubrics for scoring narratives.

The goal of *Narrative Writing* is to make students proficient at writing narratives—autobiographical, biographical, and fiction. This book assimilates easily into existing curriculum and enhances the writing program. Sharpen those pencils and turn on those word processors—the joy of writing stories awaits!

Standards for Writing
Grades 3–5

Accompanying the major activities of this book will be references to the basic standards and benchmarks for writing that will be met by successful performance of the activities. Each specific standard and benchmark will be referred to by the appropriate letter and number from the following collection. For example, a basic standard and benchmark identified as **1A** would be as follows:

Standard 1: Demonstrates competence in the general skills and strategies of the writing process

Benchmark A: Prewriting: Uses prewriting strategies to plan written work (e.g., uses graphic organizers, story maps, and webs; groups related ideas; takes notes; brainstorms ideas)

A basic standard and benchmark identified as **4B** would be as follows:

Standard 4: Gathers and uses information for research purposes

Benchmark B: Uses encyclopedias to gather information for research topics

Clearly, some activities will address more than one standard. Moreover, since there is a rich supply of activities included in this book, some will overlap in the skills they address; and some, of course, will not address every single benchmark within a given standard. Therefore, when you see these standards referenced in the activities, refer to this section for complete descriptions.

Although virtually every state has published its own standards and every subject area maintains its own lists, there is surprising commonality among these various sources. For the purposes of this book, we have elected to use the collection of standards synthesized by John S. Kendall and Robert J. Marzano in their book *Content Knowledge: A Compendium of Standards and Benchmarks for K–12 Education* (Second Edition, 1997) as illustrative of what students at various grade levels should know and be able to do. The book is published jointly by McREL (Mid-continent Regional Educational Laboratory, Inc.) and ASCD (Association for Supervision and Curriculum Development). (Used by permission of McREL.)

Language Arts Standards

1. Demonstrates competence in the general skills and strategies of the writing process

2. Demonstrates competence in the stylistic and rhetorical aspects of writing

3. Uses grammatical and mechanical conventions in written compositions

4. Gathers and uses information for research purposes

Standards for Writing
Grades 3-5 *(cont.)*

Level II (Grades 3–5)

1. **Demonstrates competence in the general skills and strategies of the writing process**

   A. Prewriting: Uses prewriting strategies to plan written work (e.g., uses graphic organizers, story maps, and webs; groups related ideas; takes notes; brainstorms ideas)

   B. Drafting and Revising: Uses strategies to draft and revise written work (e.g., elaborates on a central idea; writes with attention to voice, audience, word choice, tone, and imagery; uses paragraphs to develop separate ideas)

   C. Editing and Publishing: Uses strategies to edit and publish written work (e.g., edits for grammar, punctuation, capitalization, and spelling at a developmentally-appropriate level; considers page format [paragraphs, margins, indentations, titles]; selects presentation format; incorporates photos, illustrations, charts, and graphs)

   D. Evaluates own and others' writing (e.g., identifies the best features of a piece of writing, determines how own writing achieves its purposes, asks for feedback, responds to classmates' writing)

   E. Writes stories or essays that show awareness of intended audience

   F. Writes stories or essays that convey an intended purpose (e.g., to record ideas, to describe, to explain)

   G. Writes expository compositions (e.g., identifies and stays on the topic; develops the topic with simple facts, details, examples, and explanations; excludes extraneous and inappropriate information)

   H. Writes narrative accounts (e.g., engages the reader by establishing a context and otherwise creates an organizational structure that balances and unifies all narrative aspects of the story; uses sensory details and concrete language to develop plot and character; uses a range of strategies such as dialogue and tension or suspense)

   I. Writes autobiographical compositions (e.g., provides a context within which the incident occurs, uses simple narrative strategies, provides some insight into why this incident is memorable)

Standards for Writing
Grades 3–5 *(cont.)*

J. Writes expressive compositions (e.g., expresses ideas, reflections, and observations; uses an individual, authentic voice; uses narrative strategies, relevant details, and ideas that enable the reader to imagine the world of the event or experience)

K. Writes in response to literature (e.g., advances judgements; supports judgements with references to the text, other works, other authors, nonprint media, and personal knowledge)

L. Writes personal letters (e.g., includes the date, address, greeting, and closing; addresses envelopes)

2. Demonstrates competence in the stylistic and rhetorical aspects of writing

A. Uses descriptive language that clarifies and enhances ideas (e.g., describes familiar people, places, or objects)

B. Uses paragraph form in writing (e.g., indents the first word of a paragraph, uses topic sentences, recognizes a paragraph as a group of sentences about one main idea, writes several related paragraphs)

C. Uses a variety of sentence structures

3. Uses grammatical and mechanical conventions in written compositons

A. Writes in cursive

B. Uses exclamatory and imperative sentences in written compositions

C. Uses pronouns in written compositions (e.g., substitutes pronouns for nouns)

D. Uses nouns in written compositions (e.g., uses plural and singular naming words; forms regular and irregular plurals of nouns; uses common and proper nouns; uses nouns as subjects)

E. Uses verbs in written compositions (e.g., uses a wide variety of action verbs, past and present verb tenses, simple tenses, forms of regular verbs, verbs agree with subjects)

F. Uses adjectives in written compositions (e.g., indefinite, numerical, predicate adjectives)

G. Uses adverbs in written compositions (e.g., to make comparisons)

H. Uses coordinating conjunctions in written compositions (e.g., links ideas using connecting words)

I. Uses negatives in written compositions (e.g., avoids double negatives)

Standards for Writing
Grades 3–5 *(cont.)*

J. Uses conventions of spelling in written compositions (e.g., spells high-frequency, commonly misspelled words from appropriate grade-level list; uses a dictionary and other resources to spell words; uses initial consonant substitution to spell related words; uses vowel combinations for correct spelling)

K. Uses conventions of capitalization in written compositions (e.g., titles of people; proper nouns [names of towns, cities, counties, and states; days of the week; months of the year; names of streets; names of countries; holidays]; first word of direct quotations; heading, salutation, and closing of a letter)

L. Uses conventions of punctuation in written compositions (e.g., uses periods after imperative sentences and in initials, abbreviations, and titles before names; uses commas in dates and addresses and after greetings and closings in a letter; uses apostrophes in contractions and possessive nouns; uses quotation marks around titles and with direct quotations; uses a colon between hours and minutes)

4. Gathers and uses information for research purposes

A. Uses a variety of strategies to identify topics to investigate (e.g., brainstorms, lists questions, uses idea webs)

B. Uses encyclopedias to gather information for research topics

C. Uses dictionaries to gather information for research topics

D. Uses key words, indexes, cross-references, and letters on volumes to find information for research topics

E. Uses multiple representations of information (e.g., maps, charts, photos) to find information for research topics

F. Uses graphic organizers (e.g., notes, charts, graphs) to gather and record information for research topics

G. Compiles information into written reports or summaries

The Writing Process

The writing process can be divided into five stages that, if followed, will result in a strong narrative. The stages of the writing process can be compared to those used in preparing a meal.

Prewriting Stage: This is the most important stage in writing. In this stage, much of the writer's thinking takes place. Some prewriting techniques include the following:

- Clustering
- Brainstorming
- Freewriting about a topic
- Completing graphic organizers

Sharing ideas, offering suggestions, and figuring out the essential elements of the narrative (characters, plot, setting, and so forth) will enable the author to write the first draft of the narrative.

Similarly, the most important step in cooking a large meal is the preparation. The cook determines the type of meal, makes a list of the ingredients and utensils that are needed, and gathers items together before beginning to cook.

Writing Stage: The author writes, getting the initial narrative on paper. Writing a complete first draft is quite an accomplishment. If the author hesitates too much during the writing stage, then he or she should question whether or not the narrative is strong enough. Remember, if effort and time have been put into the prewriting stage, then the narrative will almost write itself!

Meanwhile in the kitchen, the chef cooks the selected recipes in order to test them.

The Writing Process *(cont.)*

Revision Stage: This is the third stage of the writing process. The author conducts a self-revision, and then asks for comments and suggestions from peers, teachers, and family. In order to revise, the author needs to be open to the opinions of others and decide what is needed to strengthen the narrative. Revising is often considered the most difficult stage, but it can also be viewed as challenging and exciting. Guided revision check sheets assist both the author and the reader through the revision process (see pages 118–119).

In the kitchen, the chef samples the fare and offers tastes to friends and family. The chef considers the tasters' comments and makes notes in the margins of the cookbook. Should any ingredient be taken out or added? Do all of the parts of the meal work well together?

Editing Stage: Take time to polish your masterpiece. Now that the manuscript is revised, check for misspelled words and punctuation mistakes. By completing the fourth stage of the writing process, the author makes certain that the narrative is not weakened by avoidable errors.

Meanwhile, in the kitchen, the taste-tested meal is in order. The invitations are sent, the table is set appropriately, and the kitchen is tidied for guests.

Publishing: This is the final stage of the writing process. This is the time to show off the narrative. Include pictures or photographs, word-process the manuscript, create a cover, and add details to make a fabulous first impression. The author should proudly share the narrative with classmates and family, taking joy in the finished product.

At dinner, the chef shines! Hardly a spot is on his or her apron, as the chef attended to every detail ahead of time. The guests are well-fed and applaud the cook.

Writing about Writing

On pages 8–9, you learned about the writing process. You also read a comparison between that process and the process of preparing a big meal. The steps in the writing process can be compared to many things that are also done in a certain order. Take each stage of the writing process—prewriting, writing, revising, editing, and publishing—and compare it to the stages of working on a hobby or other activity. Write complete paragraphs. Try to use smooth transitions between paragraphs so that the reader can easily understand the steps. When you are finished, illustrate the steps to go along with your written narrative.

You may consider writing about the writing process and one of the following:

- Putting on a play
- Sporting event
- Building a house
- Gardening
- Running a marathon
- Graduation
- Recital
- Science experiment
- Throwing a party
- Artistic creation
- Championship
- Bathing a pet

Activity

Use the space below to prewrite your ideas about how your chosen activity is similar to a step in the writing process.

Step 1 (prewriting):_____

Step 2 (writing): _____

Step 3 (revising):_____

Step 4 (editing): _____

Step 5 (publishing):_____

Guide to Writers' Tools

Teachers often want to know the difference between each of the following items that are in use in many classrooms:

- Journals
- Notebooks
- Portfolios

Read about each of these writing tools and include them in your narrative writing program.

Journal

Each student keeps a personal and private writing journal. The writing journal holds the student's thoughts, opinions, responses to journal questions, freewrites, and writing they may or may not choose to share. The writing journal assists students in assembling thoughts, as it allows them to express their true feelings and innermost thoughts without the fear of their words being judged or graded. The writing journal gives all students a chance to participate in writing without worrying about whether they will be called upon to share their work.

Teachers should check writing journals periodically. Students can fold back any sections that they do not wish the teacher to read. The teacher checks the writing journal solely to make sure the students are, indeed, writing.

Writing Notebook

The writing notebook can become an important part of the writing classroom, because it can house all of the prewriting exercises, notes, clusters, brainstorms, plot jots, 5W+H questions (who, what, where, when, why, and how), ideas, story beginnings, sketches, and doodles. It can also be the place to make students aware of their individual needs in spelling, punctuation, and grammar.

The writing notebook is the spot for first drafts, second drafts, etc. If one is used, it should be mandatory that it is brought to each writing class. Encourage students to choose his or her own writing notebook, however, as it is an extension of the self, a special place containing the individual's words, voice, and stories.

Writing Portfolio

The writing portfolio is a folder that is designed by the student and contains all of his or her final narratives. With computers an integral part of most schools and many homes, printing more than one copy is easy—one copy can be kept at school and one can go home. The writing portfolio may travel through the grades with the student to assess writing progress and to allow writing teachers to assess the student's skills before each school year begins.

What Is Narrative Writing?

Use this material to guide a discussion with students about the nature of narrative writing.

A narrative is a story containing specific elements that work together to create interest for not only the author but also the reader. Narratives encourage the reader to feel as if they are a part of the story, as if the story is being told directly to him or her. Narratives enable readers to "jump inside" the story and experience what the characters are doing or what is being done to them. Narratives have intriguing plots that make readers wonder, "What will happen next?" Narratives contains conflict and dilemmas, and the resolution is important to the reader. Narratives contain vivid settings that capture the imagination. Narratives have themes, messages the readers take away with them long after the stories have been read.

Discuss or review with your students each of the following basic elements of narratives.

Plot

- Plot is the who, what, where, when, why, and how outline that gives the narrative direction.
- What is the story about?
- Events unfold as they happen.
- Plot is the frame of the narrative.

Characters

- Characters are the people, animals, or inanimate objects who are affected by the actions or who are the cause of certain events.
- Characters, real or imagined, should be brought to life through the narrative.
- If characters are not portrayed or described well, the narrative will not be believed.

Setting

- Setting is where the narrative takes place.
- The setting allows the readers to visualize the scenes and the characters in those scenes.
- Remember, although a setting may be clear to the author, the author must create a picture for his or her readers.

Conflict

- Conflict is the problem that must be overcome or resolved so the readers (not to mention the main character) are not left hanging.

What Is Narrative Writing? *(cont.)*

Theme

- Theme is the message of the narrative.

- After a narrative is finished, readers should think about the story and determine its purpose.

- Nearly every narrative has a theme.

Style

- Style is the figurative language, sensory imagery, vivid verbs, strong sentences, dialogue, and point of view that makes each author unique. If each student was given the same topic to write about, each story would be different because of the style and techniques of each student.

Remind students that we live in a world where oral language is most commonly used to communicate. We rely heavily on spoken communication. The development of oral language quickly led to the telling of stories. With the creation of the written word came the ability to preserve the stories.

Inspire students to write by telling them that through writing down our stories, we are saving our personal memories and imaginings. Think of what has happened to you thus far in your life. Think about all of the people who have influenced your life or the lives of others.

What makes writing more difficult than simply telling a story aloud is that all of the facial cues, gestures, voices, accents, and movements now need to be captured with words. If the author writes a story containing the phrase ". . . and he stomped his feet like this," the reader would not be able to see the character's movements. If a person stood in front of the individual and orally shared the story, it would be easy to show how the character stomped his feet.

This is the challenge of narrative writing. This is what makes writing rewarding and powerful. Everything must be told through words, with the author as the source of the power.

The Basic Plot of Narrative Writing

When the writing process is followed, and you know your direction, a strong narrative may well explode onto the paper and be worth saving! To write a gripping narrative, you need to follow the basic plot outline. Read the chart below. Then read a piece of narrative writing that either your teacher has assigned or one of your own choosing. Notice whether or not these elements are present in what you have read. If any of the elements are missing, do you think the piece of writing might be improved by their addition?

Plotting a Well-Constructed Narrative

Beginning

- enticing opening to capture the readers' interest
- setting revealed
- main characters introduced
- conflict presented

Middle

- characters attempt to resolve conflict(s) or problem(s)
- action progresses sequentially, step by step

Climax

- the turning point of the narrative
- reveals the process involved for solving the conflict(s)

End

- tells how the resolution of the conflict(s) have affected the characters
- no new characters or plot ideas introduced
- theme or message understood by reader

Personal Narrative Questionnaire

Complete the following questions in order to get to know yourself as a writer.

1. Where do you get ideas for writing? _____

2. Where do you like to write? _____

3. Are you able to write . . .

   in the classroom? _____

   while watching television? _____

   on demand? _____

4. What *genre* (type) of narrative do you like to read most? Be sure to give a minimum of two reasons why. (Genres include: science fiction, fantasy, survival, mystery, horror, comedy, realistic fiction, children's, fairy tales, drama, western, historical, nonfiction, etc.)

   _____

   _____

5. List three ideas you have right now for fictional narratives.

   _____

   _____

   _____

The following two items will help you think about characters about whom you might like to write.

6. List three people whom you know who interest you. Include at least one reason stating why you find these individuals interesting.

   _____

   _____

   _____

7. List three people whom you do not know who interest you. Include at least one reason stating why you find these individuals interesting.

   _____

   _____

Brainstorming

Brainstorming is one technique used in the prewriting stage. Often a topic is assigned, and you look at a blank piece of paper and think, "What will I write about?" Brainstorming answers this question, because brainstorming is a way of thinking of ideas. Brainstorming is writing a list of ideas, thoughts, or words about a particular idea in your writing journal. Your brain is unleashed, and whatever it thinks of should be written down. The best ideas and thoughts often come from brainstorming. Somewhere in the brain ideas are brewing that deserve written expression.

Once an idea is generated for a narrative, you may wish to brainstorm further to gather more ideas and reflections.

The activities on this and the following page should be completed in your writing journal to create an idea bank when you are stumped for ideas. The activities may be conducted individually, or as a class. Using several pieces of chalk, several people can brainstorm on the board at once.

Activities

Each of the following topics can be brainstormed to gather various ideas. For the topic "school," you could, for example, brainstorm what you like and don't like about school or a particular subject and reasons why, what could be done to improve the school, how you learn, qualities of teachers that inspire you, etc. Each writing class may begin with brainstorming to prepare for the writing.

- School
- Winter
- Parties
- Athletes
- Environment
- Money
- Teachers
- Food
- Hobby
- Assignments
- Country
- Writing
- Fall
- Holidays
- Stars

- Politics
- Family
- Month
- Book
- Sport
- News programs
- Fashion
- Homework
- Spring
- Restaurants
- Home
- Reading
- Racism
- Day of the week
- Television show

- Athlete
- Animals
- Trends
- Summer
- Weekends
- Friends
- Town/City/State
- Exercise
- Endangered animals
- Artists
- Movie
- Star
- Period in history
- Careers

Clustering

Clustering is a way of visually organizing words and phrases about a topic. Think of the cluster as a group, or bunch, of ideas that reflect one central idea. Clustering can be compared to free association, where the brain freely creates connections between ideas. That is, if the topic is "friendship," your first thought might be "enemy," or it might be the name of your best friend. This first thought leads to other thoughts. Let your mind guide the cluster to give you many options for the narrative, helping you to relive experiences so that you can share them with others.

Activity

Cluster any word below, using the "Cluster of Grapes" on page 18. Add any words that interest you, either on this sheet or in your writer's notebook.

Ideas for Clustering

- Friendship
- Prejudice
- Rain
- Homework
- Food
- Desert
- Family
- Hatred
- Snow
- Teachers
- Country
- Violence

- Mother
- Love
- Vacation
- Weekend
- City
- Peace
- Sibling
- Fear
- Money
- Writing
- Mountain
- Music

Cluster of Grapes

Use this sheet to cluster, or gather together, any ideas that are assigned or that you choose. Begin by writing the selected word, phrase, or topic in the center "grape." Then complete the bunch of grapes by thinking of other words, ideas, thoughts, or images that relate to the word in the center. Fill in as many "grapes" as you can, so that you have many ideas from which to pick and choose when you are ready to write your narrative.

Writing a Paragraph

When writing narrative paragraphs, events usually are told from beginning to end or in *chronological* order. The story events unfold as they really happened. This helps the reader to understand the sequence of events that lead to the conclusion. Use the following activities to learn to think in chronological order while writing an interesting narrative.

Create a Concluding Sentence

For the following narrative paragraph, write a concluding sentence. Share the sentence with your classmates and discuss the variations. Then, revise the entire paragraph, adding specific details such as sights, sounds, smells, etc., to make the narrative paragraph worth reading.

My best friend Dana has a blackberry field in her backyard.

I was excited, for I had never been blackberry picking.

We got two containers and went into the blackberry patch.

The blackberries were huge and ripe.

Our fingers hardly touched the blackberries, and they would ooze delicious juice.

We held the containers under the briars, and let the blackberries fall into the bowl.

Possible concluding sentence: _____

_____

Creating a Topic Sentence

For the next paragraph, brainstorm a possible topic sentence. Share with classmates and discuss the variations.

Possible topic sentence: _____

_____

The thorns were sharp and protected the biggest blackberries.

Beehives hid in the tangled blackberry branches.

The briars grabbed our clothes and pierced our skin.

I never knew blackberry picking was so dangerous!

Extension

Use the Airplane Banner graphic organizer on page 20 to help you prewrite about the events for a narrative in chronological order.

Airplane Banner

Use the banner below to record changes in a main character, to identify or think about parts of a narrative, or for prewriting a narrative.

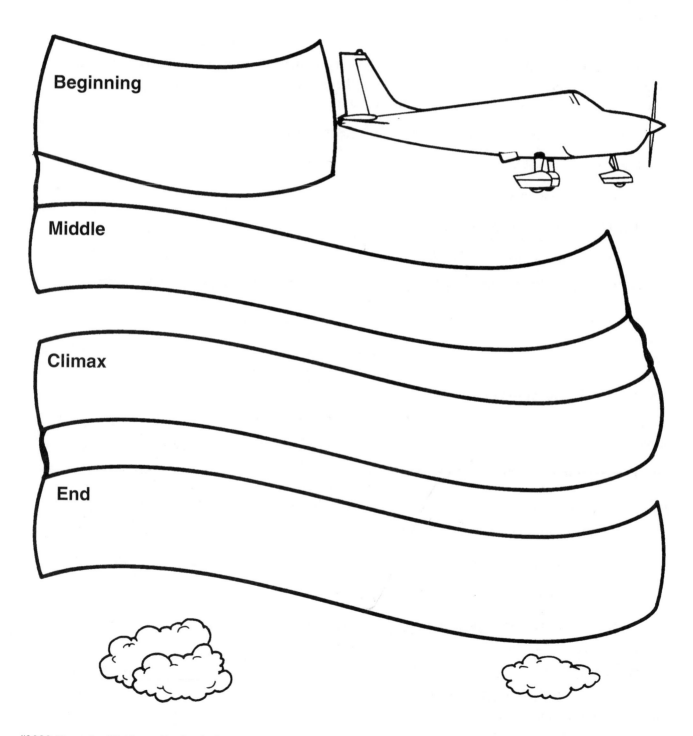

What Are Transitions?

When writing a narrative, transitions are words or phrases that smoothly carry the reader from one idea or event to the next. Transitions help the reader keep track of what is happening in the story. You don't want your reader scratching his or her head as they read your work because they are lost! Transitions help make the story logical so that the reader has some idea of where the story is going and can follow along to the story's conclusion.

Transitions can be words or phrases that connect ideas and thoughts.

furthermore, also, in addition, plus

Transitions can help the reader understand the time frame between events.

first, second, next, after, before

Transitions help the reader understand the sequence of events.

earlier, later, during, meanwhile, at the same time, simultaneously

Transitions compare and contrast ideas:

certainly, in fact, undoubtedly, indeed, as well

Transitions summarize ideas and events.

ultimately, finally, in conclusion, consequently, in the end

Activities

1. Circle the transition words in the following paragraph. As a class, determine the type of transition word or phrase that is being used.

   Last autumn when the first leaves fell, I raked the yard even though the trees were still covered with leaves. First, I grabbed the rake from the shed and began my mission. I raked and raked until I thought my arms would fall off. Eventually, I had a huge pile directly under the slide of my tree fort. My older sister told me I was too old to play in the leaves. However, she joined me once she saw the pile I made. For the rest of the day we enjoyed the fall weather. We had leaf fights, played "Catch the Falling Leaf," and also collected the most beautiful leaves to save. It's funny, but it took a pile of leaves for my sister and me to realize that we could get along.

   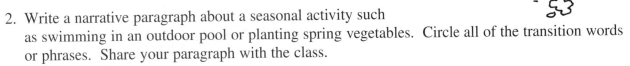

2. Write a narrative paragraph about a seasonal activity such as swimming in an outdoor pool or planting spring vegetables. Circle all of the transition words or phrases. Share your paragraph with the class.

3. Practice using computer technology by word-processing your paragraph. Use the underline feature to highlight any transition words.

Varying Sentence Structure

As you revise one of your pieces of narrative writing, notice how each of your sentences begins. Are your sentences all the same, with each one starting with a noun followed by a verb? Such writing can be dull for the reader. One way to fix this problem is to look at each sentence and decide what part of the sentence needs emphasis, or is the part that you most want the reader to notice or think about. Review each of your sentences and ask, "What do I want to say first to get—and keep—the reader's attention?"

Here are examples of how this can be done, using the same sentence in each case. Read the following sentence:

The lost child glanced up each aisle in the busy grocery store, looking for her mother.

The sentence begins with the subject, *the lost child*, and is followed by the verb, *glanced*.

Here is the same sentence emphasizing the verb or action:

Glancing up each aisle, the lost child looked for her mother in the busy grocery store.

And here is the same sentence emphasizing description:

In the busy grocery store, the lost child glanced up each aisle looking for her mother.

Each sentence structure slightly changes the meaning for the reader. The activities on page 23 can help you realize how sentence structure can be varied.

Varying Sentence Structure *(cont.)*

On page 22, you learned about varying your sentence structure and putting emphasis on the parts of the sentence you want your reader to notice. These activities can help you learn how to write or revise your sentences to add variety to your writing.

Part I

Read each of the following three sentences. Determine how each sentence is structured. Then, revise the sentence, emphasizing first, the subject; second, the verb or action; and third, the description or adjectives. Your teacher can write all of the various responses on the board or overhead to demonstrate to you and the class that there is more than one correct way to revise the sentence.

1. The red balloon floated into the cloud-filled sky.

    Revision 1: _____

    Revision 2: _____

    Revision 3: _____

2. Swinging his axe, the woodsman chopped down a tree to use for his log cabin.

    Revision 1: _____

    Revision 2: _____

    Revision 3: _____

3. In the cool shade, the elderly man rested in his hammock and sipped pink lemonade.

    Revision 1: _____

    Revision 2: _____

    Revision 3: _____

Part II

Choose one sentence from above and write a narrative paragraph using it as the topic sentence. Add four sentences to add details to your topic sentence and a concluding sentence to create a brief story.

Topic Sentence: _____

Supporting Sentences:

Sentence 1: _____

Sentence 2: _____

Sentence 3: _____

Sentence 4: _____

Concluding Sentence: _____

Combining Sentences

When you revise a piece of narrative writing, you should notice sentence length. Short sentences can add snap to a piece that contains many long, detailed sentences. On the other hand, sometimes what is needed is to combine short sentences to make one strong sentence.

For each group of sentences below, write one sentence that includes all necessary information. Add description to strengthen the sentence even more. Your teacher may write various student responses on the board so that you can discuss the differences and get ideas of how to revise your own work.

Grandpa read the newspaper.
Grandpa drank his coffee.

_____

_____

She liked picnics.
She liked exploring.
The hiker enjoyed nature.

_____

_____

The teachers went to the school assembly.
The students went to the school assembly.

_____

_____

She took out her blanket.
It was blue and white checks.
She put her basket on the blanket.

_____

_____

The children visited the museum.
It was a class field trip.

_____

_____

Caroline chose a nice spot.
It was near a brook.
It was peaceful.

_____

_____

The kittens were playful.
The kittens chased balls.
The balls had bells in them.

_____

_____

A crane came to the building.

The crane had a wrecking ball.

The crane knocked down the building.

People watched it crumble.

_____

_____

Expanding Sentences

Strong narratives have strong sentences. A strong sentence is a sentence that is descriptive, keeps reader interest, and appeals to the senses. A strong sentence builds on the previous sentences and keeps the pace of the narrative going. One way to create strong sentences is to expand, or add to, the sentences during revision. Consider the following sentence:

The horse walked.

Certainly, it is a sentence. The word *horse* is a specific noun, and the verb shows action. However, through expansion techniques, the sentence can be transformed into a fabulous, detailed sentence.

1. Describe the horse._____

2. Describe the horse's actions. _____

3. Appeal to the senses:

   I see:_____

   I hear: _____

   I taste:_____

   I touch: _____

   I smell: _____

4. Describe where the sentence takes place (setting): _____

5. Describe when: _____

6. Use strong verbs, specific nouns, and vivid adjectives: _____

Now, if you added every response, you would have quite a long, though thorough, description of "The horse walked." You need to choose the details that are worth keeping and improve your ordinary sentence.

Write down three revisions for the sentence, *The horse walked.*

   Sentence 1:_____

   Sentence 2:_____

   Sentence 3:_____

Share your revisions with the class. Discuss how the ordinary sentence becomes unique and personal. Your teacher may write various sentences on the board for you and your classmates to discuss. Then make a final revision of your expanded sentence and illustrate it.

Extension

Word process some of your sentences. Practicing using the cursor and the Cut and Paste features of your word processor to change the descriptive language in your sentences.

Expanding Sentences Template

Original sentence _____

Describe the subject of the sentence. _____

Describe the actions of the subject in greater detail. _____

Appeal to the senses.

    I see _____

    I taste _____

    I touch _____

    I smell _____

    I hear _____

Describe the setting. _____

Describe when the action took place. _____

Add figurative language by using specific nouns, strong verbs, and vivid adjectives:

Revised sentence 1: _____

_____

Revised sentence 2: _____

_____

Revised sentence 3: _____

_____

If your teacher wishes, he or she can assign you to choose one expanded sentence, and further develop it into a complete narrative paragraph. Word-process your paragraph and publish it by displaying it on a classroom bulletin board.

Choosing Strong Verbs

When writing a narrative, you need to think about the power that verbs have in your sentences. Strong verbs create a picture in the readers' minds. The readers become engaged in your story.

Read the sentences that follow and think about the verb in italics. Choose a stronger verb for each sentence from the box of vivid verbs. For each sentence, think of at least two other verbs (synonyms) that could also make the sentence more effective. Share your revised sentences with your class.

Vivid Verbs

cheered	whispered	galloped	examined	gripped
chugged	swayed	sizzled	whimpered	admired

---

1. The girl softly *called* out her answer to the math problem.

   Stronger verb:_____

   Synonym 1: _____

   Synonym 2: _____

2. The audience *called* loudly when the play began.

   Stronger verb:_____

   Synonym 1: _____

   Synonym 2: _____

3. For the experiment, we *saw* the mealworms and noted changes.

   Stronger verb:_____

   Synonym 1: _____

   Synonym 2: _____

4. The horse *went* around his corral.

   Stronger verb:_____

   Synonym 1: _____

   Synonym 2: _____

Choosing Strong Verbs *(cont.)*

5. The baby sadly *called* for his mother.

   Stronger verb:_____

   Synonym 1: _____

   Synonym 2: _____

6. At the museum, I *liked* a portrait of two brothers.

   Stronger verb:_____

   Synonym 1: _____

   Synonym 2: _____

7. The old tree *moved* in the breeze.

   Stronger verb:_____

   Synonym 1: _____

   Synonym 2: _____

8. Crossing the street, a mother tightly *held* her son's hand.

   Stronger verb:_____

   Synonym 1: _____

   Synonym 2: _____

9. The bacon *cooked* in the pan.

   Stronger verb:_____

   Synonym 1: _____

   Synonym 2: _____

10. With the car out of gas, the driver *turned* into the service station.

    Stronger verb:_____

    Synonym 1: _____

    Synonym 2: _____

Extension

Word process each of your 10 revised sentences. Use the italics feature to highlight your vivid verbs.

Cut or fold under before reproducing.

Answers

1. whispered
2. cheered
3. examined
4. galloped
5. whimpered
6. admired
7. swayed
8. gripped
9. sizzled
10. chugged

Standards and Benchmarks: 1A, 1B, 1C, 1D, 2A, 2B, 2C, 3A, 3B, 3C, 3D, 3E, 3F, 3G, 3H, 3I, 3J, 3K, 3L

Improving the Use of Verbs

Assign one or more of the following activities to give students practice using well-chosen verbs. Remind them that verbs add power to their writing by creating action in the reader's mind.

The Playground

Students will draw a picture of their dream playground. Students can then write ten sentences containing strong verbs about what happens at the playground. To create a challenge, tell students that each verb can only be used once. To use technology, have students word process their sentences and highlight the action words in different colors. Create a bulletin board of dream playgrounds and sentences containing vivid verbs.

The Kitchen

As a class, brainstorm a list of appliances and gadgets found in the kitchen. For each object, students should think of at least one action verb the particular appliance, gadget, or tool has the ability to do. Students should choose three objects, illustrate them in action, and brainstorm five action verbs for one of the illustrated objects.

I Said, You Said

The word *said* is overused, especially when writing dialogue. As a class, brainstorm a bulletin board of verbs showing the many ways words can be spoken. Have students add to the bulletin board as new words are thought of. Students should have a special page in their writing notebook for all of their new words for *said*. When assigning projects containing dialogue, allow the word said to be used only once in a piece of writing.

Standards and Benchmarks: 1A, 1B, 1C, 1D, 1H, 1I, 1J, 2A, 2B, 2C, 3A, 3B, 3C, 3D, 3E, 3F, 3G, 3H, 3I, 3J, 3K, 3L

What Time Is It?

When writing a narrative, it is important to tell your story in chronological order. When you write what happened first, second, third, etc., reader confusion is avoided.

What do you do during a 12-hour period? For this activity, you will choose the day of the week and a month. (The month is important; you would not shovel snow on the same day that you pick tomatoes.) Then choose a verb for each hour of the day, writing them around the clock. You must not repeat any verbs. Then write a brief sentence using each verb. Here is an example using a school day.

Day of the week: Friday

Month: September

12 hours in the life of John:

Counts — Guzzles — Hurries
Pledges — 11 12 1 — Plods
10 — 2
Rushes — 9 — 3 — Cheers
8 — 4
Chomps — 7 6 5 — Races
Washes — Awakens — Gulps

Around-the-Clock Sentences:

John awakens for school.

John washes his face.

John chomps on toast.

John rushes for the bus.

John pledges allegiance to the flag.

John counts lunch tickets.

John guzzles his juice.

John hurries through his work.

John plods through his math.

John cheers the school bell.

John races to the bus.

John gulps a glass of milk.

Verb Clock Template

For your "verb clock," you should pick a day of the week, month, and twelve-hour period. Next to each verb, include your one-sentence description including the verb, as in the sample on page 30.

Day of the week:

Month:

12 hours in the life of: _____

(your name)

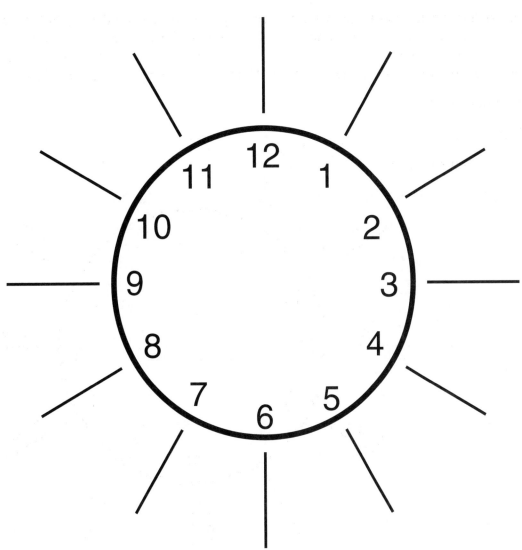

Extension

1. Exchange "clocks" with a classmate. Write a character sketch based on what that person does in a 12-hour period.

2. Respond to the following question in a well-developed paragraph: *If you were a clock, what kind would you be, and why?* Consider the following: mantle clock, grandfather clock, digital clock, alarm clock, pocket watch, wristwatch, designer watch, athletic watch, waterproof watch, etc.

3. Write a narrative using no less than a three-hour time frame from your clock.

Adjectives

Adjectives are the describing words that add important details to the nouns in your writing. Adjectives can add information about shape, size, color, mood, and so forth. Underline all of the nouns in the following sentences. Revise sentences to include one strong adjective before each noun. Share your revisions with your classmates and discuss how the sentences change according to the adjective used.

1. The girl ran down the sidewalk. _____

_____

2. The frog hid under a mushroom. _____

_____

3. Dribbling down his chin was sauce. _____

_____

4. A balloon floated into the sky. _____

_____

5. The truck rumbled onto the road. _____

_____

6. Fruit ripened in the basket. _____

_____

7. Frightened by the noise, the children cried. _____

_____

8. The sun and wind dried the clothes. _____

_____

9. The boys and girls laughed at the magician. _____

_____

10. In the office, a nurse tended to the child. _____

_____

Description Riddles

Practice writing complete descriptions by writing riddles about a variety of topics. Use the brainstorming ideas on page 16 to give you some ideas for objects to describe. Write the riddle on the front side of a folded piece of paper. On the inside, give your answer and illustrate the object. Be sure to use accurate adjectives in your description riddles. Before you write, try these riddles for fun:

Riddle #1

I am a great ball of fire. I paint a new picture on my canvas before retiring each night. Sometimes I fight the clouds with my paintbrushes, and they let me have some space. When I turn off my light, people turn on theirs.

What am I? _____

What other descriptions could you add to this riddle?

Riddle #2

I carry lazy people to their destinations, for I never tire. People push my buttons all day, but I don't get upset. When I do, an "out of order" sign is placed on me, and boy, do some people get angry! My doors open and close, open and close, and I never become confused about where I am, or what floor I'm on. I guess you could say I'm pretty smart. The stairs get jealous, but hey, that's just too bad.

What am I? _____

What other descriptions could you add to this riddle?

Riddle #3

I may look like the real thing, but I am not real. My eyes are glassy but never cold. I am furry but not fierce. I get tangled up in the sheets sometimes, but I am rarely forgotten. I was named after a famous president.

What am I? _____

What other descriptions could you add to this riddle?

Cut or fold under before reproducing.

Answers

1. sunset   2. elevator   3. teddy bear

Description Riddles *(cont.)*

Brainstorm a list of nouns that you could describe in a riddle:

People	Places	Things
_____	_____	_____
_____	_____	_____
_____	_____	_____
_____	_____	_____
_____	_____	_____
_____	_____	_____

Choose one item from each column and write a riddle on the front of a folded piece of paper. On the inside of the paper, write the answer as well as an illustration or picture of your chosen subject. Share your riddles with classmates.

Person: _____

Riddle: _____

_____

_____

_____

Place: _____

Riddle: _____

_____

_____

_____

Thing: _____

Riddle: _____

_____

_____

_____

Sequencing Events

Writing a cause-and-effect narrative can help you learn to organize events chronologically, or in the order in which they occur. The following narrative is based on the book *If You Give a Mouse a Cookie* by Laura Joffe Numeroff. Read and discuss the narrative below with your classmates.

The Gardener

If you give a gardener a shovel, he'll ask for dirt. When the gardener sees the dirt, he'll ask for flowers. When he sees the flowers, he'll ask for a hose. When the gardener turns on the hose, he'll take a drink of water. After the drink, he'll wipe sweat from his brow. Now, the gardener has a smear of dirt across his face. The dirt reminds the gardener of his shovel. And, of course, the flowers that need to be planted.

Activities

1. Compose a cause-and-effect narrative of your own.

2. Add adjectives to the narrative to make it more interesting.

3. Word process your story and then copy it onto a disk. Create two versions of your story. In the first version, use the bold feature to highlight the nouns and the underline feature to highlight the adjectives. In the second version, choose and print out your story in a font (typeface) that you think adds meaning to your story.

4. Read books by Numeroff. Write a story in a similar style and illustrate it to create a picture book.

Seeking All Adverbs

There are plenty of adverbs in the narrative below. Your assignment is to seek them out, circle them, and then complete the activities that follow.

An Island Adventure

Yesterday, a boy was stranded alone on an island. He had been quietly fishing in a very small rowboat when a thundercloud suddenly appeared from nowhere. Soon, a bolt of lightning swiftly fell downward, shattering his rowboat. Luckily, the boy had his life jacket on, and he quickly managed to grab an oar. Next, amidst turbulent waves, the boy floated aimlessly, barely able to keep his head above water for what seemed an endless journey. Finally, the storm ended, and the sun miraculously shone, causing the water to become still. The boy shouted happily, "Land! There! Land!" The boy somehow found the strength to paddle to shore. Now here he was, on a strange, deserted island far from home. The boy shook terribly and desperately cried out. He was ravenously hungry and completely exhausted. He knew that in order to act wisely, he had to devise a plan—a plan to survive.

Activities

1. How many adverbs did you find in your search?

2. Reread the story without the adverbs. What happens?

3. Write a one-page ending to "An Island Adventure" that includes a minimum of 20 adverbs. Write your one-page continuation first, without thinking about adverbs. Then, as you revise, circle all the adverbs. You may be surprised to see how many adverbs you already have! Word process your final draft, using the underline feature to highlight the adverbs in your ending.

5W+H Questions

Answering the *5W+H questions* (who, what, where, when, why, and how) provides the basic information needed to begin a story. By answering the 5W+H questions, you can determine whether you have enough ideas to write a strong narrative.

Completed narratives can also be revised using the 5W+H technique. After reading a narrative, answer the following questions:

- Who was in the narrative?
- Where did the narrative take place?
- Why did the characters do what they did?
- What was the narrative about?
- When did the events happen?
- How was the conflict resolved?

The following activity will help you learn to use the 5W+H technique for your own writing.

Party Time!

As a class, discuss the following invitation. Notice that it answers the 5W+H questions.

Event: Winning the Soccer Championships

Who: All Junior League soccer players and fans

What: Make your own pizza, ice cream sundae bar, indoor swimming, volleyball, basketball, and organized games

When: Saturday, November 18, 12–4 P.M.

Where: All-Sport Athletic Club, Soccerville

Why: The Junior League soccer players won the trophy and want to celebrate with those who cheered them on all season!

How: Bring towels, bathing suits, and a smile!

Activity

Create three invitations for three separate events. All invitations must include answers or responses to the 5W+H questions: who, what, where, when, why, and how.

Brainstorm a list of events first, for example:

- baby's birth
- graduation
- new home or apartment
- retirement
- promotion
- anniversary

Illustrate or decorate your final invitation and post a copy on an "Invitations" bulletin board. Read the bulletin board and discuss the event you would most like to be a part of, and the event that seems the least appealing.

The Plot Jot

In the prewriting stage, when an idea finally hits, a good idea is to complete a "plot jot" in your writing journal. To jot means to write a quick reminder word or phrase that can prompt you as you create a first draft. When you write a plot jot, you quickly write down the basic outline of the story.

Once the idea is on paper, it's time to put the plot jot to work. Read your plot jot. Read it again. Before you decide whether or not the idea is worth saving, ask yourself the 5W+H questions (see page 37) based on the plot jot. Have a classmate, relative, or teacher read your plot jot and ask three more questions about it. Respond to these questions. See where your answers lead the narrative.

The plot jot that follows serves as an example of how one can be created and used.

Art Class

Everett liked art class.

He enjoyed making projects

Everett couldn't wait to finish his project.

It was for his brother's birthday.

When he got to the art room, Everett couldn't believe what happened.

Neither Everett nor his brother would forget this birthday!

As a class, brainstorm questions about the plot jot. Write these questions on the board:

- Why does Everett like art class?
- What kinds of projects does Everett make?
- What is Everett's favorite art activity?
- Who is Everett's brother? How old is he? Do they get along?
- What is Everett making for his brother's birthday? Why?
- Will his brother like it?
- Why can't Everett believe what happened in the art room?
- What happened?
- What will Everett's brother think?
- Why won't this birthday be forgotten?

Remember that even though all questions should be answered, not all answers need to be used in the narrative. Why? Because some information may be unnecessary or lack interest for the reader.

Writing an Alphabet Narrative

When writing a narrative, you need to tell what happens in the order in which it occurs, or chronological order. When your narratives are in chronological order, you help your readers understand what happened first, second, third, etc.

For fun and practice, write a narrative using the alphabet as a guide. Starting with the letter **A**, write the first sentence of a fiction or nonfiction narrative. (See the example below.) Try to use all 26 letters of the alphabet to help you write the events in chronological order. A dictionary is helpful when writing an alphabet narrative.

As a class, read the sample alphabet narrative below. Then, individually or as a class, finish the narrative, beginning with the letter **L**. Brainstorm a list of titles and select one that fits the narrative. Share your version of the alphabet narrative with the class.

A All my life, I wanted to do something my brother couldn't do.

B Because he is much older, its hard to find one thing he can't do.

C "Computers," I thought, "Maybe I can be better on the computer!"

D Delighted, I read all I could about computers.

E "Entertaining" is not an adjective I would use to describe computer manuals.

F Frustrated, I felt defeated.

G "Great," I muttered.

H "How can I be better at computers if I can't understand the computer manuals?"

I I wondered what else I could do.

J Jinxed is how I felt.

K Keeping my wits about me, I decided to find something else to be good at.

Extension

Write your own alphabet narrative on a topic of your choice, beginning with the letter **A**. Word process your narrative and give it a decorative border before printing it.

Standards and Benchmarks: 1A, 1B, 1C, 1D, 1E, 1H, 1J, 2A, 2B, 2C, 3A, 3B, 3C, 3D, 3E, 3F, 3G, 3H, 3I, 3J, 3K, 3L, 4A

Note to teacher: Make two copies of this chart for the follow-up exercises to the narrative "Field Day."

Sensory Imagery

Using the five senses—seeing, hearing, touching, tasting, and smelling—when writing narratives stimulates the senses of your readers. They feel included in the narrative because you have appealed to their senses. When you describe what you see, hear, taste, touch, and smell, your readers draw upon their senses and become involved in the story.

Activity

Read the narrative on pages 41–43 and record all of the sensory imagery on the chart below. Be aware that some descriptions may appeal to more than one sense. Share your results with the class.

Sensory Imagery Chart

Sight	Sound	Touch	Smell	Taste

Field Day

Field Day is the most awaited and anticipated day of the school year. Rain or shine, Field Day is a chance to compete and win—for yourself, your homeroom, and your grade.

In P.E., the Field Day events are introduced and practiced weeks ahead of time so that no time is lost explaining the rules. Our sneakers squeak on the gymnasium floor, our black soles leaving long black tracks that serve as stop-and-go points for relays. We compare the lengths of the marks, believing that the longest mark is a prediction of who will win on Field Day. Angry voices and harsh words claiming the longest and darkest marks cause the alarming shrill of the coach's whistle. He reminds us that not everyone has black-soled sneakers, and it may be that phantom mark, the invisible track, that we need to fear.

Field Day is real. It is no longer a practice. It is our Olympics. On Field Day, our sweat is different. It is the scared sweat, the I-want-to-win sweat, the sweat that is from the unforgiving June sun. Our parents wave from the sidelines; our classmates depend on us. A patch of goldenrod cheers the racers and throws pollen confetti at the contestants.

Practice sessions aren't nearly as exciting as actual Field Day. A feeling close to the night before your birthday, when for once you haven't snooped and don't know what you are getting. Your fingers cross for luck beneath cool, crisp, clean sheets that have a scent of fresh air that can't be found in the classroom. Soothing night noises nuzzle you to sleep, and when you awaken, traditional school clothes are tossed aside for clothes in your homeroom's designated color: fire engine red, sunny mustard yellow, and "I surrender" white.

You dress and go to breakfast, but you are unable to finish a piece of cinnamon-raisin toast. You somehow manage to guzzle a cold glass of orange juice and are rewarded with an extra boost of energy. Let the games begin!

Field Day *(cont.)*

In the three-legged race, the feel of hot, itchy burlap against your bare legs makes you hop faster toward the finish line. The smells of dirt and freshly mown grass linger after the wheelbarrow race, and soil sinks under dull fingernails. Around the field, pairs of figures are tripping, falling, and laughing. They are also wishing their teammate and best friend wasn't three inches taller or shorter or 10 pounds lighter or heavier.

Then it's on to the dashes. Expectations soar higher than the flags waving on the field before the individual 50- and 100-yard dashes. Volunteers have timed all homeroom members, and the names of the winners from each homeroom are placed on the clipboard. These winners then compete to be the fastest sprinter, the Mercury of the entire school. All cheer their homeroom representatives as the final races begin. Sometimes, the school record is broken, and the winner's name is engraved on a gold plaque that holds the names of the other Field Day 50- and 100-yard dash champions since Field Day began at our school.

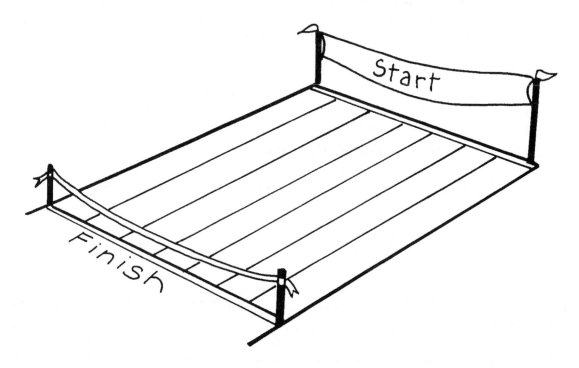

Blue, red, and yellow ribbons are awarded. Certificates with each student's name are presented, signed by the principal and the P.E. teacher. But they might as well be signed by the President, that's how wonderful the certificate feels in your hand. The ultimate reward, though, may be the free ice pop, the best one you've ever tasted. Many times you've asked your mom or dad to buy the Field Day ice pop at the grocery store, but these ice pops aren't sold anywhere. They aren't sold by ice cream trucks, and you can't order them online. They come in cardboard boxes from the school cafeteria freezer, are labeled "Field Day Ice Pops," and are only available once a year.

Sticky, red popsicle juice streams down, running a race on your forearm as you eat. You glance around the field, a rainbow of T-shirts merge into one. Everyone has a popsicle—teachers, students, parents. There is no team, no one shining star. On Field Day, everyone wins.

Field Day *(cont.)*

Discussion Questions

1. Identify some uses of imagery in "Field Day." How does the imagery make the narrative more enjoyable to read?_____

_____

_____

_____

_____

2. What is the conflict in "Field Day"?_____

_____

_____

_____

_____

3. What is the theme, or message, of "Field Day"? _____

_____

_____

_____

_____

4. Add a description to "Field Day" using each of the five senses. Share your sentences with the class._____

_____

_____

_____

5. In your writing journal, write about a Field Day or similar experience in which you have participated.

Extension

Word process your narrative from Step 5 above. Use the graphics feature to add a border to your finished piece.

Original Sensory Imagery

Note to teacher: You will need copies of page 40 to complete the activity below.

From the following list of places, choose one to think about with sensory descriptions. (You can also choose your own place.) Record your ideas on a blank copy of the chart on page 40. You can complete a similar chart for other topics any time that you are in the prewriting stage of the writing process and need a place to record your ideas.

Once you have completed the chart, develop a narrative paragraph or essay appealing to all five of a reader's senses. Share your narratives with classmates.

Places

- Party
- Farm
- Museum
- Barbershop
- Room in house
- Beach
- Restaurant
- Movie theater
- Playground
- City
- School
- Laundromat
- Fair
- Mall
- Construction site
- Doctor's office
- Friend's house
- Parent's office

- Dog's or cat's favorite spot
- Lake
- Canyon
- Planetarium
- Fossil or rock shop
- Toy store
- Computer store
- Market
- Airport
- Zoo
- Train station
- Grandparent's house
- Your room
- Bird or fish store
- Park
- Garden or nursery
- Factory
- Alley

Personal Sensory Awareness Chart

Complete the following drawing to understand and appreciate your own senses. Use the drawing to help you create a "facial collage" of your likes and dislikes. Write a narrative based on your collage and share it with your classmates.

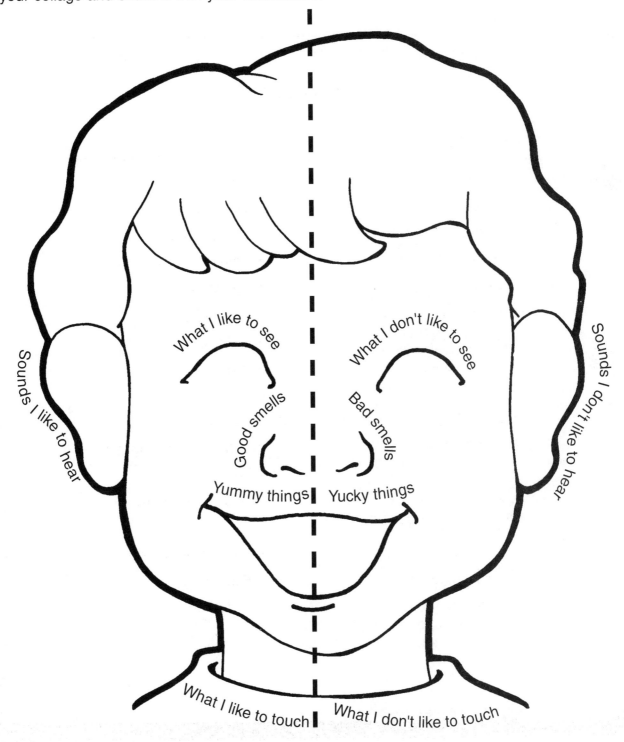

Conflict

What is *conflict*? Conflict is a problem that makes you think about the correct action to take in a tough situation. Conflict happens when someone has difficult personal choices to make or when someone disagrees with another person or situation.

In narrative writing, conflict is the obstacle or problem that the main character is trying to overcome. Without conflict, narratives usually become boring.

When there is conflict at the beginning of the narrative, the reader is immediately drawn into the story. The reader wants to find out how the character deals with the conflict, and if he or she is able to resolve the conflict favorably—that is, in a way that satisfies the character. The reader may also learn something from the narrative about solving similar conflicts in his or her own life.

Think about your favorite books, television shows, or movies. What was the obstacle, or conflict, that the characters faced? Sometimes, there is even more than one conflict, and as one conflict is resolved, another one presents itself.

Think about the conflicts that are in your life. Conflicts can be small (like deciding what you should have for breakfast) or serious (like not completing a writing assignment). While the conflicts may be very different, either one can be the basis of a narrative that is full of energy. When you use conflict in your narrative writing, it makes your writing more powerful and your reader more satisfied when the conflict is resolved at the climax, or turning point, of the narrative.

Can you recall a story that really gripped your attention? Chances are good that you were vitally interested in the story because of the conflict. While the characters, setting, and plot are important story elements, conflict is what sets the story in motion. Don't be afraid of conflict. Even admirable characters have tough decisions to make or have to confront difficult people or situations.

Types of Conflict

There are many types of conflict that people encounter in their lives. Under each type of conflict labeled below, there is a story passage that illustrates its use. Can you think of a time when you experienced a similar problem? Keep your notebook or journal nearby as you read so that you can capture any ideas that you may have. Notice, too, as you read that there can be many different types of conflict in a story.

Person versus Self

One month ago, Abby was assigned a book to read and prepare a book report on. But has Abby completed the task? No, Abby has watched TV quiz shows, talked on the phone, and surfed the Web instead. Now the report is due tomorrow.

Person versus Person

Abby calls her best friend, Meg, and asks for help completing the book report. Meg begins to offer suggestions and then asks, "Abby, what's the title of the book?" Abby doesn't know the answer. Her friend hangs up in disgust.

Person versus Society

Abby pleads for her mother to take her to the library, but when they arrive, Abby finds it has closed. Abby leaves a message on the librarian's answering machine, demanding longer hours. She vows to start a petition on this issue after she completes the book project.

Person versus Machine/Technology

Abby plunks herself at the computer and goes online to find a chat buddy who has read the novel. Abby is foiled when her system crashes.

Person versus Nature

Abby tries to remember where she was exactly when she lost her book. She remembers sitting on a bench outside her building, and she rushes downstairs. Alas, all that is left is the cover, pinned under the bench by rain and bleached by the sun. At least Abby now knows the title.

Activity

1. Finish the narrative about Abby. Choose one or more of the conflicts and write a resolution for it. Then give the narrative a title.

2. Brainstorm a list of conflicts you have faced, especially those at school. Choose one conflict and cluster about it. Identify the conflict type, and how the conflict was resolved. Write a brief narrative about it and share it with the class.

Personal Conflict

Brainstorm a list of personal conflicts you have experienced with family, friends, and school. Use this list to provide ideas for future narratives.

Subject	Conflict	Resolution
Self versus Family		
Family versus Family		
Family versus Society		
Family versus Machine		
Family versus Nature		
Self versus Friend(s)		
Friends versus Friends		
Friends versus Society		
Friends versus Machine		
Friends versus Nature		
Self versus School		
School versus School		
School versus Society		
School versus Machine		
School versus Nature		

School Subjects and Conflict

As a class or in small groups, brainstorm a list of conflicts and conflict types that you find within various school subjects. For example, in health, a conflict is the fight against cancer. The type of conflict is person versus nature, as people conduct research to cure this illness. Try to find a least one conflict for each conflict type. If you are working in small groups, report your conflicts to the class.

Subject	Conflict	Type of Conflict
Math		
Science		
Social Studies		
Health		
Art		
Music		
Physical Education		
Computers		
Reading		
Language Arts		

Extension

Write a narrative about one of the conflicts you discovered in a subject area. Revise and word process your final draft and share it with the class.

Current Events and Conflict

Use this sheet to record local, state, national, and world events that contain conflicts. Describe each conflict and assign it a type (see page 47). Track the conflicts on a weekly and/or monthly basis to find out whether or not they were resolved and, if so, how.

Type of Conflict:

Conflict

Event:

Event:

Event:

Event:

Event:

Facing Our Problems

Read and respond to the following questions in your writing journal.

- What do you do when faced with a problem? Do you seek advice? If so, from whom? Do you keep your problem to yourself? Do you wait for something to happen, or do you take charge, attacking the conflict head-on?

- When there is conflict, is it important to you that you win the conflict, or do you just want to end it in any way possible? Does it depend on the type of conflict or the people involved?

- Think about a conflict that was not resolved to your satisfaction. Can you think of some other ways that you could have spoken or acted that might have changed how the conflict ended? Write a narrative about the conflict that includes your new ideas. Imagine how the conflict might have ended if you had acted or spoken in this new way.

- In one paragraph, write down what you do most often when faced with a problem. Show your actions with an illustration. Add your paragraphs and illustrations to a bulletin board titled "How We Face Our Problems." As a class, discuss the positive and negative ways of resolving conflicts.

- You may wish to invite the school guidance counselor or a similar person to your class to discuss conflict resolution. Ask that person about some ways to resolve conflict so that everyone wins or feels satisfied about how the conflict ends.

- Is it possible to solve every conflict? Discuss this idea with your classmates. What is the thing to do if a conflict cannot be resolved?

Family Advice

Interview two family members, asking them to share two conflicts, one in which the conflict was resolved in his or her favor, and one in which it was not. For each conflict, you should ask how the person handled the conflict, and if he or she wishes the conflict had been handled differently. Ask each family member you interview for his or her advice on how to handle new conflicts. Write about this advice in a narrative about these family members. Revise and edit your story; then word-process it on the computer.

Person interviewed: _____

Relationship: _____

Conflict satisfactorily resolved: _____

_____

Type of conflict: _____

Conflict not satisfactorily resolved: _____

_____

Type of conflict: _____

What does the person believe could have been done to resolve the conflict satisfactorily?

_____

_____

Person interviewed: _____

Relationship: _____

Conflict satisfactorily resolved: _____

_____

Type of conflict: _____

Conflict not satisfactorily resolved: _____

_____

Type of conflict: _____

What does the person believe could have been done to resolve the conflict satisfactorily?

_____

What Would You Do?

Determine the type of conflict in each scene below, and then write what you would do in the same situation. Then compare the scene below to a personal experience. Use the Rainbow Comparison Graphic Organizer (page 83) to sort out your ideas. Share your suggestions with classmates. Remember, there is no right answer.

❖　　❖　　❖

A school dance will be held this Friday. My parents have made it clear that I can't attend school dances until high school. I was invited to sleep over at my best friend's house on Friday. Her parents will take us to the dance, and I could go to the dance without my parents knowing.

Conflict type:_____

What would you do? _____

_____

_____

❖　　❖　　❖

My dog bit our neighbor, and she has started a petition stating that dogs should be banned from our complex. My parents said our dog has to go. But I've had Sam my whole life!

Conflict type:_____

What would you do? _____

_____

_____

❖　　❖　　❖

On the first day of school, everyone on the school bus made fun of the bus driver because he had big ears. I didn't make fun of him, because he's my Uncle. I didn't say anything to the other kids, and when I got off the bus, I ran into the school.

Conflict type:_____

What would you do? _____

_____

Standards and Benchmarks: 1A, 1B, 1C, 1D, 1E, 1H, 1I, 1J, 2A, 2B, 2C, 3A, 3B, 3C, 3D, 3E, 3F, 3G, 3H, 3I, 3J, 3K, 3L

Conflict Anonymous

Write below about a personal conflict that has not yet been resolved. Do not sign your name! Your teacher will assign to you a number to put on your paper instead of your name and will keep a record of your name and number. He or she will collect the papers and put them into a notebook. You and your classmates can read each other's anonymous papers and write advice on the back of the sheets. After a week or so, the teacher will hand back the papers to their owners so that the advice can be read.

My personal, unresolved conflict: _____

_____

_____

Conflict type: _____

Best advice: _____

_____

_____

Worst advice: _____

_____

_____

What I am going to do about my personal conflict: _____

_____

_____

What actually happened: _____

_____

_____

Should I have acted differently in confronting this conflict? _____

_____

_____

_____

Conflict Hurdles

Use this sheet to organize a narrative that contains 2–3 conflicts. How did you or the person about whom you are writing jump over the hurdles or resolve the conflicts as they happened? How were the conflicts resolved in the end?

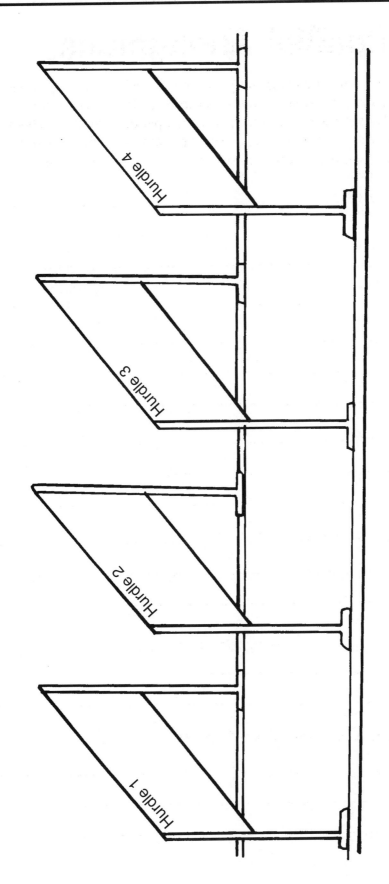

Understanding Themes

It is difficult to write a narrative that does not have a theme. A theme is a message that is revealed in the story. The theme may be stated directly, as in fables in which the moral is told at the conclusion. A theme may also be indirect, leaving the reader to decide the story's message. There can be more than one theme for a narrative.

Common themes often are similar to the well-known messages that are found in proverbs, or sayings such as "Honesty is the best policy." As a class, brainstorm on the board a list of proverbs that can become the basis for themes in your narratives. Discuss the fact that most proverbs have both a literal and a figurative meaning. "Literal meaning" refers to the meaning that the proverb actually states; "figurative meaning" refers to the underlying meaning that the proverb suggests. For example, "Look before you leap" literally means that for safety reasons you should look ahead before you jump. Figuratively, this proverb means to think ahead about the consequences of your actions.

Here are some proverbs to discuss and to get you started in brainstorming others:

The early bird catches the worm.	What goes around comes around.
Too many cooks spoil the broth.	Don't cry over spilt milk.
Don't judge a book by its cover.	Don't put all your eggs in one basket.
A rolling stone gathers no moss.	Small people can do big things.
Work before play.	Practice makes perfect.
He who lies down with dogs wakes up with fleas.	Don't be deceived by appearances.
People who live in glass houses shouldn't throw stones.	Good things come in small packages.

Activity

Choose two proverbs from the list above or your brainstormed list. Write about a personal experience that reflects this proverb and that could be used to develop the theme of a personal narrative.

Proverb: _____

Personal Experience: _____

_____

Proverb: _____

Personal Experience: _____

_____

Theme-Related Activities

Assign one or more of the following activities to students.

1. Students can read children's picture books and summarize the plot, using the 5W+H technique. Then, the students can each identify at least one theme and support their opinions. Students can share their opinions and discuss other themes that may apply to the narrative.

2. Students can create a bulletin board of themes and proverbs.

3. Based on the brainstormed list of themes, students can each choose one a day to write about a personal experience that reflects the theme. All of those entries become ideas for personal narratives.

4. Students can each read newspaper and magazine articles, present a summary of the article, and state its theme.

5. Students can analyze advertisements and identify the message the company is attempting to convey. Students can locate advertisements and present the ads and "themes" to the class.

6. Students can read short stories and identify their themes. If they are advanced students, they can write about how the story conflict and plot relate to the theme as well.

7. Assign the graphic organizer on page 58 to help students organize their thinking about a theme for a narrative.

Theme Balloon

When you write a narrative with a strong theme, you need to make statements and reveal actions that support your ideas and opinions. Use each section of the balloon to organize your thoughts on a theme about which you care.

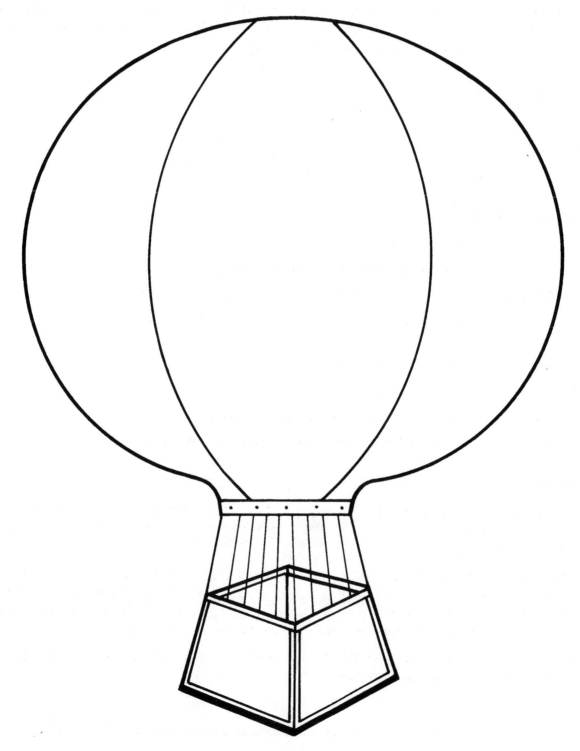

Standards and Benchmarks: 1A, 1B, 1C, 1D, 1E, 1H, 1J, 2A, 2B, 2C, 3A, 3B, 3C, 3D, 3E, 3F, 3G, 3H, 3I, 3J, 3K, 3L

Different Points of View

Who is telling the story? The most authentic voice you can use for narration is your own. Why? Because when you write from your own point of view, it is the most familiar, natural way of telling a story. No one else can get inside your head like you can! You know your feelings and reasons for your actions, and when you write from this point of view, your story is believable and honest. Sometimes, experimenting with other points of view is fun, challenging, and allows for creativity. Here are the points of view that are used most often in narrative writing.

First person point of view

- "I" as the narrator

- Most often used in telling personal accounts

  Example: I will never forget the day my hamster died. . . .

Third person point of view

- "He," "she," "it," "they" perspective

- Written as if the story is observed from outside the characters

- Reader must guess the feelings of characters by their actions and words

  Example: He pounded his fist against the wall and screamed, "Let me out!"

Third person omniscient point of view

- "He," "she," "it," they" perspective

- Narrator can write about the thoughts and feelings of characters

  Example: She called him a liar, though she knew he was telling the truth.

Activities

1. Rewrite the following passage three times, using first person, third person, and third person omniscient points of view. Be creative, but don't change the basic idea of the passage. Share your points of view with the class.

   Three students are eating their school lunches in the cafeteria. Their teacher comes to the table and states, "This is your new classmate. I thought you all would give an appropriate welcome." The teacher leaves the table, and the new student stares at the school-bought lunches surrounding the brown bag lunch he has set down on their table with his trembling hands.

2. When you have written and edited the exercise, word process it on the computer three times, choosing a different font for each point of view.

Standards and Benchmarks: 1A, 1B, 1C, 1D, 1E, 1H, 1I, 1J, 1K, 2A, 2B, 2C, 3A, 3B, 3C, 3D, 3E, 3F, 3G, 3H, 3I, 3J, 3K, 3L

No Words Needed

When Max told me—floppy-eared Charlie—that I was his best friend, his best buddy in the whole wide world, I knew that I was lucky. Of course, I knew I was special to Max, but hearing the words whispered so that no one else could hear them made them more meaningful. I like to think of myself as Max's protector, although sometimes I think Max feels he is protecting me. In friendship, sometimes you have to compromise—you have to let the other person think or believe something so he or she isn't hurt.

For instance, take Grandma's beef stew. It's this brown sloppy beef broth with mushy carrot chunks, peas the color of army trucks, and enough onion to make your tears fill a fishbowl. Mom loves it. Dad loves it. Anna-Marie likes to push buttered bread in the stew and ends up eating half a loaf of bread. Max, however, hates it more than fluoride dental treatments. One lick of the stew, and Max asks for a bowl of cereal. He knows he won't get the sugary, after-school cereal, but he doesn't care. Give him a bowl of bran, and Max will eat that over Grandma's beef stew.

Let me get to my point. Max believes I enjoy the beef slop. He gives his to me, and I lop it up. Ooooh, agony! What carrots and peas do to my digestive system seems not to bother Max or the rest of my family, and because I finish Max's bowl, guess what: lucky ol' Charlie gets to lick clean the rest of the Millers' stew bowls. Truth? I hate Grandma's beef stew more than I hate my annual visit to the vet, but I eat it for two reasons. First, I eat it so Max doesn't have to, and second, I eat it so the good table scraps keep coming my way.

The next issue is the cellar. The cellar is a creepy, dark place that forces my tail between my legs. Max keeps his train set in the cellar. Even though I don't play with the trains and get scolded if my paws hit the tracks or knock over a tree, since I'm Max's best friend, I "S-T-A-Y"

No Words Needed *(cont.)*

right beside Max, both eyes open, always on the lookout for monsters or spiders. Even though the train whistle coming out of the tunnel sounds like the boom-boom of fireworks and scares me into a heavy pant, I stay. Because of my fear, I let out a low growl, trying to be top dog. Max sometimes growls back at me, and when he does, I put my paws over my face so he doesn't see my eyes laughing. Max's growl is a pathetic one that wouldn't even frighten the neighbor's house cat, but I don't let on to Max. And I don't let on that I am S-C-A-R-E-D of the cellar, either, because then he might think I'm not his protector.

How I feel about the garbage man and his rumbling truck is quite different from the way Max views him. Max thinks the garbage man is a good guy who takes away rubbish—leftover food even I won't eat, used tissues, empty boxes, lousy story beginnings, and who knows what else. But to me, the garbage man is a bad guy, a thief who steals the smells belonging to the Millers' home. He inhales our odors, admires our trash, and throws it in his monstrous machine that sounds like exploding fireworks. Each time I hear the rumbling of the refuse truck, I cringe. My fur bristles and the wolf-like roar inherited from my ancestors causes Max to say, "Oh, Charlie, relax, it's just the garbage man." Just the garbage man!

Another misinterpretation Max has is the definition for school. To me, school deprives Max of eight hours of romping playtime with me. Some days, Max returns home from school happy. Other days, sad. Still others, angry, frustrated, or on top of the world. What kind of place is school to make you feel so many different emotions? I'm glad I don't have to go to school. School makes me lonely. Usually Max wants to go to school.

What's so good about school that makes Max not mind being away from me for one, uh, fourteen, er, fifty-seven—ah, okay, so I can't tell time!

None of our differences matter, though, because our definition for friendship is the same. No need for words, just being together. You be my pillow one day, I'll be your pillow the next. Understanding, trust, love. Sure, Max has other friends, and I play with other canines occasionally, but I always run back to Max. I smile every time I hear him call, "Char-leeeeee, home!"

No Words Needed *(cont.)*

Discussion Questions

1. When did you realize that the narrator was a dog? Find the clues in the narrative that let you know that Charlie is a canine. _____

   _____

   _____

   _____

2. How do figurative language and sensory imagery bring the narrative alive? Give examples. _____

   _____

   _____

   _____

3. What is the theme of "No Words Needed"? _____

   _____

   _____

   _____

Activities

1. Rewrite one section from the narrative from Max's point of view. Share it with the class.

2. Think of one person, place, or thing for which a pet may have a different definition for friendship than its owner. Write about the pet and owner definitions and share them with the class. Use the chart on page 63.

3. Brainstorm the qualities of friendship. Write a narrative explaining why these qualities are important.

4. Word-process your narrative about friendship and add it to your writing portfolio.

Standards and Benchmarks: 1A, 1B, 1C, 1D, 1E, 1H, 1I, 1J, 2A, 2B, 2C, 3A, 3B, 3C, 3D, 3E, 3F, 3G, 3H, 3I, 3J, 3K, 3L

Pet and Owner Dictionary

Create a dictionary of definitions or meanings of terms for yourself and for a pet. For example, to you winter may be "a cold season of the year," but for a dog, it may mean "getting out the embarrassing plaid dog sweater," while for a canary, it may mean "the time when the so-called friends that live in the tree outside the window leave me behind." Fill in the chart below to get you started on your dictionary. Add three of your own words to define on a separate sheet of paper.

Type of Pet _____

Term	Owner Definition	Pet Definition
Television		
Summer		
Friends		
Music		
Weekend		
School		
Food		
Money		
Chores		
Leisure time		
Sports		

Extension

Make a booklet in which to create a final copy of your original dictionary. Use a real dictionary as a guide for proper entry format. Include a creative title reflecting the contents of the dictionary, such as "Chirp the Cockatiel's Meanings of Life." Use the draw program on your computer to create illustrations to include in your dictionary.

Annual Family Letter

It's that time of year again! It's time to send warm holiday wishes to friends and relatives. This year, you have been chosen to write the annual family letter that will let those you don't often see know what you and your family have done, or not done, over the past year. Write your family holiday letter in third person point of view by following the steps below:

1. Brainstorm your most vivid memories over the past year. Have family members do the same. Compare lists and discuss. Consider your audience. Who will your annual family letter go to? As a family, come up with 4–6 events that you will share in the annual family letter.

2. Cluster the term "holiday greeting." What does the sending and receiving of cards, other family letters, and yearly photographs mean to you?

3. Arrange the family events in chronological order.

4. For the final presentation, scan family photographs onto the letter, create a *PowerPoint™* slide presentation of the past year, and e-mail the letter to the family and friends who have e-mail addresses.

Figurative Language

Figurative language is the use of descriptive words that bring the reader into your story. The figurative language that you use also makes your writing unique. Review the following terms and definitions. Think about how the second sentence in each example is strengthened with the use of figurative language.

Simile

A simile is a comparison between two unlike things, using *like* or *as*.

> Her smile was wide.

> *Her smile was so wide it looked like a piano keyboard.*

Metaphor

A metaphor compares two unlike things without using *like* or *as*.

> The boy enjoyed playing imaginary games like knights and dragons.

> *The boy was a Golden Knight, protecting his little sister from the fire-breathing dragon that lives in the sand box.*

Personification

Personification assigns human characteristics and traits to nonhuman objects.

> The students did not know the answer to question number three.

> *The pencil fought furiously with the eraser, battling over question number three.*

Hyperbole

Hyperbole is the use of gross exaggeration to describe something that could never happen in real life.

> The teacher's voice was so loud the students across the hall could hear her.

> *The teacher's voice was so loud the astronauts orbiting Earth could hear her chant, "Noun equals person, place, or thing."*

Alliteration

Alliteration is the repetition of two or more sounds.

> The witch told us to be careful at midnight.

> *The witch's washed-out, withered lips whispered, "Watch what awaits you at the bewitching hour!"*

Onomatopoeia

Onomatopoeia is a word that imitates a sound.

> I like to listen to the wolves at night.

> *I like to hear the wolves howl at the still moon.*

Playing Hooky

"Yeah!" Cooper threw his cordless phone on his comforter as if he were throwing the winning touchdown pass and admired his reflection. "Kaylan said yes!" Cooper flexed his muscles—mountains that would rival the biggest in Colorado. "Then again, who wouldn't say yes to Adonis? Wait until Kaylan sees me tomorrow. I'll blind her with my good looks. I'll burn a hole in the dance floor. Kaylan will melt and be mine forever!"

The time on Cooper's alarm clock warned, "Come to bed, Cooper, my man." The shades were unrolled to blanket the windows. Cooper rolled up like a burrito in his tan blankets and drifted into dreamland.

"Wake up, Rip Van Winkle," Cooper heard his mother's voice. "Come on, Coop, you'll be late for school." Cooper's head felt like a cinder block. "Coop, rise and shine! Someone named Kaylan called. She said she was meeting you early to study for the math test."

"Um." Cooper was Rip Van Winkle. Kaylan, test? Kaylan, dance? When he tried to sit up, all he could see were six blurry images of his mother gathering a thousand dirty socks. "Ugh." The groan gurgling in the hollow pit of his stomach turned into a ferocious beast and slammed him against the headboard.

"Cooper, you don't look well." He felt his mom's hand on his forehead. "You're on fire! Stay put, honey. I'm getting the thermometer."

Playing Hooky *(cont.)*

The thermometer had barely touched his lips when the mercury became a torpedo, rocketing up through the glass. "Cooper, you're staying home today. No school. No math test. No dance."

No dance! The words echoed through his head like a shout across a valley. Even though Cooper's head was an overfilled balloon ready to pop, Cooper's mind whirled like a tornado. "No, Ma. It's nothing a couple of aspirin won't cure."

Abandoning Kaylan was not part of his plan. But Cooper's eyelids were ten-pound barbells, and his throat shrieked with each swallow. Cooper had been bitten by the flu bug. Its stinger had silently slipped under Cooper's sheets while he slept, and its venom had stolen Cooper's health. Cooper's first dance with the girl of his dreams was ruined.

Pink medicine thick as tar bubbled in the teaspoon, teasing, "I taste like bubble gum!" Cooper's teeth were pried open and the medicine dribbled down his throat, nauseating every taste bud. His swollen eyes sank into his skull faster than the setting sun, and he felt as if he had walked for a million years in the desert without water. As the medicine traveled through Cooper's veins, searching for the flu bug, it left a trail of pink medicine that would trap the bug if it tried to escape before it was destroyed.

The pile of tissues on Cooper's blanket was a snowy ski slope that would reach the moon if Cooper's nose kept running like it was in a slalom. The trumpeting sound that blasted from his nose rivaled that of a snow blower. Momentarily, the slalom stopped. When his nose resumed its race, Cooper tenderly touched its tip with a tissue and begged, "Please, stop running!"

His mother brought a tray of chicken soup, fizzy ginger ale, and crackers coated with salt—the standard sick menu, with free delivery. The carrots floated on the soup's surface like people overboard awaiting rescue from the sea. "Save me!" Cooper heard the carrots cry.

Playing Hooky (cont.)

"Save you?" Cooper questioned. "Save me!"

The telephone ding-a-linged and pierced Cooper's ears even worse than the drummer that had been banging and pounding cymbals all day in his ear canal. The resonating telephone bell sounded like the end-of-school signal, his alarm clock, and the entire block's car alarms all in one. Cooper knew he would explode if the phone wasn't answered.

"Hrgh?" Cooper croaked. He covered the receiver and cleared his throat with mighty effort. "Hello?"

"Hi, Cooper?" an angelic voice asked. Momentarily, Cooper thought he was being called to Heaven. "It doesn't sound like you."

"It's not. I mean it is. I have the flu." Cooper's raspy voice answered.

"It's Kaylan. I heard you were sick." Who needed pink medicine when you had a girl like Kaylan calling you?

"Yes. Sorry about missing our study session." Cooper didn't know how he would say that he couldn't go to the dance.

"That's okay," Kaylan sighed.

"And my mom," it was always best to blame bad things on parents, "says that I can't go to the dance." Kaylan tried to speak, but Cooper interrupted. "I mean, I wouldn't be much fun. Actually, Santa called and asked if I could guide his sleigh." Cooper paused, listening to Kaylan's soft, sparkly laugh. "But maybe if I get better over the weekend we could meet somewhere and study."

"Cooper, I—" Kaylan began.

"No biggie," Cooper's stomach erupted like a volcano. How could he expect a girl like Kaylan to forgive him for ditching her? A girl like Kaylan gets asked by every guy in the school. She probably had a waiting list of dates.

"Cooper," Kaylan finally shouted, "be quiet! You keep interrupting me! I got bitten by the flu bug, too. I left school early and missed the math test. In fact, so many kids left school that the dance was canceled." Kaylan sneezed. Then her voice softened. "It's been rescheduled for next Friday. Think you'd want to go with me?"

"Wow." Cooper smiled. Never before had Cooper simultaneously smiled and been sick. A girl like Kaylan had the power to do that.

Playing Hooky *(cont.)*

Discussion Questions

1. How does figurative language enhance "Playing Hooky"? _____

_____

_____

_____

2. Identify the conflict and type of conflict in "Playing Hooky." _____

_____

_____

_____

3. What are the possible themes of the narrative? _____

_____

_____

_____

4. Do you think "Playing Hooky" is a good title? Can you think of another title? _____

_____

_____

_____

Activities

1. Find at least three examples of each of the following figures of speech. Write your discoveries on a separate sheet of paper.

   - simile
   - metaphor
   - personification
   - alliteration
   - hyperbole
   - onomatopoeia

2. Cluster the word *flu* in your writing notebook. Then make a list of figures of speech on the left side of your writing notebook. (Use the list in Activity #1, above.) For each figure of speech, think of at least two original phrases or sentences describing how you feel when bitten by the flu bug. Finally, write a narrative about the flu. Share it with the class. Use any comments about your narrative to revise it. Then word-process a final copy of your narrative.

3. Describe a typical sick day. Use a time line to organize your day and schedule.

4. Is there a "Kaylan" or "Cooper" in your life? In your journal, write about this person.

Standards and Benchmarks: 1A, 1B, 1C, 1D, 2A, 2B, 2C, 3A, 3B, 3C, 3D, 3E, 3F, 3G, 3H, 3I, 3J, 3K, 3L

Clichés: "Old as the Hills" Similes

The following similes are overused, or *clichés*. Create new sentences that are original similes with the same meanings as clichés and share them with the class. The first one has been done for you as an example:

Cliché: Her hat was as old as the hills.

Original: Her hat was so worn that the rose on its brim looked like yellowed newsprint.

1. Smart as a fox

   Original sentence: _____

2. Blind as a bat

   Original sentence: _____

3. Strong as an ox

   Original sentence: _____

4. Sleeps like a baby

   Original sentence: _____

5. Looks like you've seen a ghost

   Original sentence: _____

6. Feels like there are butterflies in my stomach

   Original sentence: _____

7. Tough as nails

   Original sentence: _____

8. White as snow

   Original sentence: _____

9. Run like the wind

   Original sentence: _____

10. Red like a lobster

    Original sentence: _____

11. Happy as a lark

    Original sentence: _____

12. Look like the cat that ate the canary

    Original sentence: _____

Sizzling Similes

Think of comparisons to complete the following sentences. Share your ideas with the class. Discuss the comparisons being made and vote on the most vivid simile.

1. At recess, the students were as loud as _____

_____.

2. During the test, the class was quiet as _____

_____.

3. He studied so late, he felt like _____

_____.

4. She forgot to bring her books home and felt like _____

_____.

5. The principal patrolled the hall like _____

_____.

6. The crossing guard looked like _____

_____.

7. When the bell rang, the students jumped like _____

_____.

8. Outside, the day was as warm as _____

_____.

9. The cafeteria looked like _____

_____.

10. During passing time, the halls sounded like _____

_____.

Standards and Benchmarks: 1A, 1B, 1C, 1D, 2A, 2C, 3A, 3B, 3C, 3D, 3E, 3F, 3G, 3H, 3I, 3J, 3K, 3L

Metaphors

Recall that a metaphor is a description that uses direct comparison. Unlike a simile, the words *like* and *as* are not used in writing a metaphor. Here is an example of a metaphor:

> *The tree was our fortress, its limbs our watch posts.*

Complete the following activities as assigned by your teacher.

Writing Original Metaphors

Use the following words in original metaphors. Illustrate each sentence and share metaphors with the class. Below is an example using the word *tears*.

spider web	skyscraper	clouds	thunderstorm
ballerina	blonde hair	the moon	desert

Her tears were dewdrops, clinging to the flower before dropping to the ground.

Emotions and Metaphors

As a class or on your own, brainstorm a list of emotions on the board or in your writing journal. Choose a minimum of three emotions, and give three to five metaphors for each emotion chosen. Use one of the emotions and one of its metaphors as a starting sentence for a narrative paragraph. Word process and illustrate your paragraph, and then share it with your classmates. Here is an example:

  Sample emotions: happiness, sadness, fear, surprise, anger, frustration.

Metaphors for jealousy:

  Jealousy is an alley cat looking through glass into a warm room.

  Jealousy is a toddler watching her big sister make muffins.

  Jealousy is a clown watching the trapeze artist in spangles dazzling the crowd.

Rainbow Metaphors

Write down the colors of the rainbow: red, yellow, blue, green, orange, and violet. Create at least three metaphors using each color. Draw your rainbow and write your sentences in it.

Abstract Metaphor

An abstract noun is a noun that you can't see, hear, taste, touch, or smell. Abstract nouns include peace, racism, unity, life, hope, forgiveness, and fear. As a class, brainstorm a list of other abstract nouns. Together with your classmates, choose one abstract noun to work on. Each student can then create at least one strong metaphor to capture any thoughts and feelings about the word. Create a collage using magazine pictures, illustrations, words, clip art, and photographs that you feel represent the word.

Personification

Personification is a technique of giving human qualities to nonhuman things. Complete one or more of the following activities to learn how to use this type of figurative language.

The Refrigerator

Brainstorm a list of what is in your refrigerator. Choose one of the items and write a narrative paragraph using at least two examples of personification. Here is an example:

> *The Swiss cheese felt its surface. It was covered with holes! Was this normal? It looked over at the block of cheddar. No telling what it looked like beneath its solid foil wrap from the store. The Swiss cheese eyed tubs of ricotta and cottage cheese. No help there. It turned around and looked at a runny slice of Brie and gasped. Maybe holes weren't so bad after all.*

The Test

Imagine you are taking a test and are stumped on question #3. Suddenly, the inanimate objects on your desk and in the classroom each take on a life of their own, jumping about and debating each other. But will they give you the correct answer to #3? Write and illustrate a narrative describing this scene. The narrative should include at least three examples of personification.

The Perfect Spot

Brainstorm ideas about a favorite spot, and then write a paragraph describing this place using the following situation: You are about to leave this special place, and the special place is doing everything in its power to make you stay. For example, if you pick the lake, imagine that the lake is inviting you back into its still, cool water and that the trees by its banks want you to rest in their shade. You should include at least three examples of personification in your paragraph and illustrate the scene.

Personification *(cont.)*

Using the setting below, choose some inanimate objects and write sentences using personification. Examples are given below.

The corn hid behind the scarecrow as protection against predators.

The tree limbs sang creaky lullabies at night.

The leaves broke free from Mother Tree to dance with the wind.

Hyperbole

Hyperbole is a gross exaggeration that could never happen.

For the following comparisons, decide whether the sentence is hyperbole or is something that is possible in reality.

I'm so hungry I could eat ten hamburgers.

I'm so hungry I could eat an elephant.

When I'm mad my head pops off.

When I'm mad my ears turn red.

The frog hops higher than the Empire State Building.

The frog hops over six lily pads.

Her smile was wider than the Mississippi River when she got her test back.

Her smile took up her whole face when she got her test back.

Write your own hyperboles here. Use one as the start of a narrative. E-mail the narrative to a friend or family member to help you with your revision. Use the word processor to make any changes in your narrative.

_____

_____

_____

_____

_____

_____

_____

_____

_____

_____

Believe It or Not

Browse through an edition of *The Guinness Book of World Records.* Decide which feats are possible and truly amazing, and which ones seem to be an exaggeration or hyperbole. Share your ideas with the class.

Then, imagine that you have been hired by the editors of a similar book to write two new entries. The entries must be hyperboles, written in the style of a truthful nonfiction narrative. There should be no way that these new entries fit into the realm of possibility.

In each entry, you must answer the 5W+H questions and then add details, using, of course, hyperbole. Entries should be written as complete paragraphs. Include an illustration or diagram, and compile the paragraphs into a class collection of new world records.

Entry 1

Who: _____

What: _____

Where: _____

When: _____

Why: _____

How: _____

Fascinating details: _____

_____

Entry 2 _____

Who: _____

What: _____

Where: _____

When: _____

Why: _____

How: _____

Fascinating details: _____

_____

Alliteration

Use these activities to practice the technique of alliteration.

Name Game

Write your name on lined paper, putting each letter on a new line. Then, write an alliterative phrase that describes you. Remember, to be considered alliteration, the sentence needs two or more words that begin with the same sound. Here is an example:

> Always awakens angrily.
>
> Needs a nap at noon.
>
> Dunks donuts for dessert.
>
> Reads by the rippling river.
>
> Everyone enjoys her elephant collection.
>
> Asks for assistance with alliteration.

Illustrate your alliterative name and post it on a bulletin board. Do one for a family member or friend!

School Spirit

Use the same technique described in the "Name Game," above, to write about your school. Share your work with your classmates. As a class, choose the best alliterative phrases or sentences from all the students' work. Using sentence strips, stenciling, or bulletin board letters, create a bulletin board in the entrance of your school.

Steven's School is Super

Famous Person Alliteration

Choose a famous person whom you admire and research at least ten facts about this individual. Write his or her full name down the left side of your paper, and use the researched materials in alliterative phrases or sentences beginning with the first letter on each line. For a final presentation, include a portrait that you have created of the famous person.

Standards and Benchmarks: 1A, 1B, 1C, 1D, 2A, 2B, 2C, 3A, 3B, 3C, 3D, 3E, 3F, 3G, 3H, 3I, 3J, 3K, 3L

Onomatopoeia

Onomatopoeia occurs when a word or words imitate a sound. Here is an example:

The dog's nails tippy-tapped on the vinyl floor.

Shoe Sounds

As a class, brainstorm a list of different types of shoes. Write the sounds these shoes make on different surfaces. Choose one type of shoe, one surface, and three sounds this shoe makes. Illustrate your chosen shoe and surface, and incorporate the onomatopoeia in your illustration.

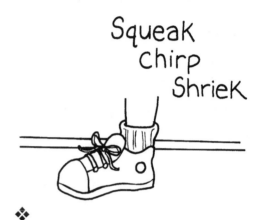

❖ ❖ ❖

Who's in the Zoo?

Brainstorm a list of animals and the noises the animals make. Design a zoo that includes 10 animals of your choosing. Create a zoo map, writing onomatopoeic sounds in the animals' cages rather than labeling them with the animals' names. See if your classmates can correctly identify what animals are in your zoo!

❖ ❖ ❖

Sound Time Line

Create a time line of sounds heard or made in a six-hour period. Be creative with your time line. Use the time line as a story starter for a narrative piece of writing.

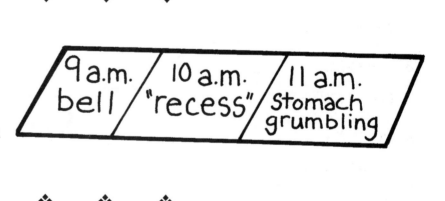

❖ ❖ ❖

Neighborhood Noise

Create a map of your home, yard, neighborhood, or town. The map should include at least five different places. Write down the sounds heard at these places. See if your classmates can identify the place you have mapped by reading the onomatopoeic words.

Adding Appropriate Sounds

For the following sentences, add onomatopoeia. Share your responses with your classmates.

1. The fire _____ and warmed the room.

2. The bicycle _____ over the autumn leaves.

3. A _____ was heard after I threw the stone into the water.

4. A loud _____ came from the barn.

5. Thunder _____ and the rain
_____, forcing me to hide under the covers.

6. The _____ from the tea kettles startled me.

7. The old jalopy _____ down the dirt road, making noises.

8. The subway _____ along the tracks.

9. The police car's siren _____ into the night.

10. The _____ of the sick boy worried his family.

11. The dog's _____
frightened the little boy.

12. The siren _____
through the town.

13. The pencil_____
across the paper.

14. Her nails _____
on the chalkboard.

15. The machine _____ as it mixed the candy.

Extension

Use your computer to word process the sentences. Put the onomatopoeic words in a font that adds fun and meaning to each word.

Characterization

When writing narrative work, it is essential to develop your characters, real or imagined. What you envision in your mind must be conveyed to your readers. Good writers will create pictures of their characters with words.

Whether fiction or nonfiction, your characters need to be realistic. To achieve this, complete a character sketch of each character. Draw a sketch of what the character looks like, too. The more realistic the characters are to you, the better chance you have of making them seem real for your readers.

When you write fiction, character sketches can help you figure out how or why a character acted the way he or she did. This is known as the character's motive. You can also compare and contrast the traits of different characters or show the relationships between them. This knowledge can help you create more engaging conflict in your stories.

Characters also fall into types. There are heroes and heroines, helpers, wise figures, villains, and fools. These types can be broken down into smaller categories: the fumbling hero, the good-hearted fool, the remorseful villain, the helper turned enemy. The trick is not to use characters that are stereotypes or characters that have as much interest as a piece of cardboard.

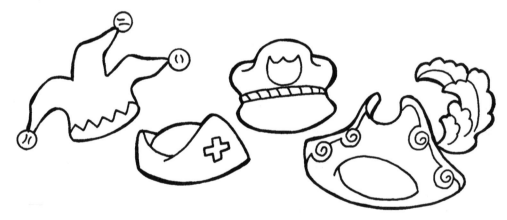

What type of character(s) do you need to think about or create for your next narrative? Your characters may be fiction or non-fiction. Write down your ideas. Use the Character Sketch Template on page 81 to help you give some bone and muscle to the characters that you would like to use.

Character Sketch Template

Use your imagination to create a character, or base your character on someone you know. Then fill in the following information to help you write a narrative. Use a separate sheet for each important character in your story.

Name _____

Date of birth _____

Age _____

Male/Female _____

Address _____

Occupation _____

Physical description

    Eyes _____

    Hair _____

    Complexion _____

    Weight _____

    Height _____

    Unique features _____

    Stature _____

    Clothing _____

Family description

    Name(s) and age(s) _____

    Relationship to character _____

    Occupation(s) _____

Home description

Best friend(s)

    Name(s) and age(s) _____

    Traits of friend(s) _____

    Personality _____

Activities for Creating Characters

Assign one or more of the following activities to your students.

Matching Game

Students should be instructed to cut out pictures from magazines of people whom they do not know. Students will analyze the picture, consider the surroundings and setting, and create a character using the Character Sketch Template (page 81). This information should be used to write a narrative description of the character. The pictures should be posted on a bulletin board, and students can read their final descriptions. The class can try to identify the correct magazine picture.

Where Did You Get Those Brown Eyes?

Students should write a character sketch on each member of his or her immediate family. The family should be enlisted to complete this task. Family members should compare traits and characteristics with each other. The final project would be for students to write a narrative about what he or she inherited or learned from his mother, father, guardian, or siblings.

My Best Friend

Students should complete a fictitious character sketch on their ideal best friend and then write a narrative about his or her friend. The narrative can be used as a tribute to present to the friend by wordprocessing it in a fancy font and decorative border. Consider putting the tribute in a handmade frame.

Calling All Super Heroes!

Students will create a superhero and villain. A character sketch should be completed on each character using the Character Sketch Template (page 81), as well as the Rainbow Comparison Graphic Organizer (page 83) to compare similarities and differences. Place the two characters in a setting and create a narrative. Will good triumph over evil?

Adjective Brainstorm

As a class, brainstorm a list of adjectives used to describe people. Create a bulletin board of adjectives that can be added to daily. Refer to the bulletin board when you need to add details to a character sketch or narrative.

Rainbow Comparison Graphic Organizer

Differences

Similarities

Differences

Use the "rainbow" to connect the sun and the rain cloud. Inside the rainbow, write similarities between the two characters to show how they are similar.

In the cloud and in the sun, write the unique traits to show how the characters are different. You can also use this organizer to look at other story elements such as setting.

Standards and Benchmarks: 1A, 1B, 1C, 1D, 1J, 2A, 2B, 2C, 3A, 3B, 3C, 3D, 3E, 3F, 3G, 3H, 3I, 3J, 3K, 3L

A Character's Refrigerator

Thinking about what is found on a person's refrigerator can tell a great deal about his or her character. Use the activity below as a springboard for writing several narrative pieces.

Activity

1. As a class, brainstorm what the magnets below could represent or reveal about a person.

For example:

- Likes bicycles

- Training for a race

- Wants a new bike

- Saving allowance and using the magnet as an incentive to save

- Likes outdoor activities

- Favorite form of transportation

- Reminds person of childhood

- Incentive to remove training wheels

2. Now, assume that all of the above magnets belong to one individual. Create a character sketch based on the four magnets on his or her refrigerator.

3. Write a one-page narrative about this person. Include how he or she came to possession of one of the magnets from above. Share the narratives in class.

4. Design three magnets that would reveal something about you. Draw the magnets and write at least three complete sentences explaining what they reveal about you.

5. Choose one magnet currently on your refrigerator. Bring it to class as a show and tell. Tell to whom the magnet belongs and what you believe it says about the person.

Extension

Visit a relative or friend and ask to look inside his or her refrigerator. Make a list of what you find. Then look on the outside and make a similar list. What does each list suggest about the person's character? Does what you find on the inside match what you find on the outside? Does the person have lots of nearly empty jars and plastic produce bags inside the refrigerator, but a magnet that reads "Neatness Counts" on the outside? Think and write about any similarities and differences that you notice.

Standards and Benchmarks: 1A, 1B, 1C, 1D, 1H, 1J, 2A, 2B, 2C, 3A, 3B, 3C, 3D, 3E, 3F, 3G, 3H, 3I, 3J, 3K, 3L

What Is a Time Line?

A time line is a visual map spanning a specific time period. A time line allows you to "see" what happens over an extended period of time. Study the time line on page 86 to see how one is constructed and to help you complete the activities below that are assigned by your teacher.

The World and Me Time Line

Create a time line like the sample provided on page 86. Determine at least six significant events in your life, and research parallel events that were current events at the time.

Personal Time Line

Create a personal time line for one 12-hour period in one day of the week. Your time line should have 12 entries, one for each hour. Analyze the time line and plan a narrative based on the time line. Include setting, characters, plot, and conflict.

Time Line of the Past

Brainstorm a list of emotions. Create a time line of your past that focuses on a single emotion that you choose, including one event from each year of your life that represents this emotion.

News Time Line

Choose one year in our history and research the news of that year. Choose one significant world, national, or current event from that year and create a time line outlining the event from beginning to end. Illustrate the time line and share it with the class.

Proud Time Line

Cluster the word *proud* in your journal, or use the Cluster of Grapes organizer on page 18. Brainstorm all of the times you have been proud in your life. Choose one of these proud times and create a time line showing the sequence of events that led up to this sense of pride. Your time line should reveal characters, plot, conflict, setting, and theme. Illustrate the time line and share it with the class.

Family Time Line

Choose one family member or couple and create a time line of their life or courtship. For example, you may research a time line showing how your parents, grandparents, or aunts and uncles met one another, dated, fell in love, and got married. Include characters, setting, conflict, and plot in your time line. Illustrate with photographs or drawings.

Autobiographical or Historical Narrative

Use a time line that you have created using one of the activities above to write a complete autobiographical or historical narrative. Read it to a partner as he or she looks at your time line. Word process both your narrative and the time line and display them together for others to read and learn about you.

Sample Time Line

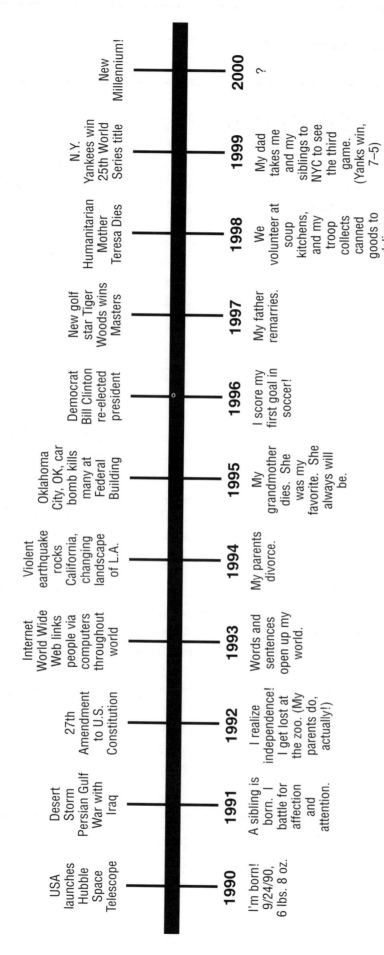

Year	World Event	My Life
1990	USA launches Hubble Space Telescope	I'm born! 9/24/90, 6 lbs. 8 oz.
1991	Desert Storm Persian Gulf War with Iraq	A sibling is born. I battle for affection and attention.
1992	27th Amendment to U.S. Constitution	I realize independence! I get lost at the zoo. (My parents do, actually!)
1993	Internet World Wide Web links people via computers throughout world	Words and sentences open up my world.
1994	Violent earthquake rocks California, changing landscape of L.A.	My parents divorce.
1995	Oklahoma City, OK, car bomb kills many at Federal Building	My grandmother dies. She was my favorite. She always will be.
1996	Democrat Bill Clinton re-elected president	I score my first goal in soccer!
1997	New golf star Tiger Woods wins Masters	My father remarries.
1998	Humanitarian Mother Teresa Dies	We volunteer at soup kitchens, and my troop collects canned goods to deliver.
1999	N.Y. Yankees win 25th World Series title	My dad takes me and my siblings to NYC to see the third game. (Yanks win, 7–5)
2000	New Millennium!	?

Activities

1. Analyze the time line. What does the time line reveal?
2. Brainstorm titles for this time line.
3. Work in small groups to research one year from the top of the time line in order to find three other significant events of that year.
4. Discuss how the top and bottom parts of the time line parallel one another.
5. Create a similar time line of your own life (see page 85, "The World and Me Time Line" activity).

Dialogue

Dialogue is the words and sentences that your characters say. Dialogue should sound like real people talking. The more dialogue you use, the faster paced and more dramatic your story will be. Dialogue can reveal many things about your characters, the setting, the plot, and the conflict.

Read the samples of dialogue below. Discuss with your classmates how each bit of dialogue reveals something about the story element heading under which it is organized.

Dialogue That Reveals Character

"If you pinch me one more time, I'll pinch you. And I don't care if you are a girl!"

"The new girl is so sweet, she gives me a bellyache. I'll bet it's an act. No one can stay nice for that long."

"See that poster on my wall? That's me in 10 years."

Dialogue That Reveals Plot

"First, let's go to the music store. Then, we'll look at earrings and grab a snack at the food court. Then, we'll get tickets for the movie."

"You told me you took the bus alone when you were nine, and I'm 12. Times haven't changed that much!"

"I think the cheerleading tryouts went well. Camp really helped—oh, sorry, you couldn't go. Didn't mean to rub it in."

Dialogue That Reveals Setting

"I don't want to ride in Uncle Fred's car. The old clunker will never make it on those hills, and I don't want to miss the party. Don't you remember what happened last year? I spent the night waiting for the tow truck in the middle of nowhere and missed the party."

"Put on sunscreen. The tropical breeze is deceiving. And here, don't forget your hat. And sit under a palm tree."

"The buildings are so tall. Skyscrapers, right? And the sidewalks tremble. Is that from the subway?"

Dialogue That Reveals Conflict

"I can't believe you, my best friend, lied."

"Will you sign my petition? The more signatures, the better chance we'll have at building a new playground."

"Dad, I know I didn't clean my room, but the guys need me. You can't have a three-on-three hoop game if only two guys show. They'll get creamed!"

Standards and Benchmarks: 1A, 1B, 1C, 1D, 1E, 1H, 1J, 2A, 2B, 2C, 3A, 3B, 3C, 3D, 3E, 3F, 3G, 3H, 3I, 3J, 3K, 3L

Dialogue Activities

Students can complete one or more of the following activities to learn how to write dialogue for their narratives.

1. Students can practice dialogue by writing and responding appropriately to each of the sample quotations on page 87. When sharing their responses, students can comment as to what is revealed through the dialogue.

2. Students can each use one of the quotations on page 87 as the first sentence of a fictional narrative. Students should first outline the narrative, using either 5W+H questions or a plot jot (see page 38). Share the narratives in class.

3. In groups, students can find examples of dialogue in children's books that reveal something about characters, setting, and conflict.

4. In groups, students can write a dialogue between a teacher and students that contains dialogue that reflects characters, setting, plot, and conflict. Students may also experiment with revealing the theme of the group dialogue narrative.

5. Students can listen to conversation at home, on the playground, on the bus, or wherever they happen to be. Students can write down the words others say that reveal characters, setting, plot/or a story, and conflict.

6. Students should tell their family members about their day and reveal in their dialogue something about the character, setting, plot, and conflict. As a model, write the following sentences on the board, and have students discuss what is revealed:

   "Mom, Jeremy finally came back to school, and I volunteered to help him catch up with the work."

   "I have a spelling test tomorrow. Will anyone quiz me?"

   "Mom, did you get your hair cut today? It really makes you look younger."

   "I'm not going to the dance because I have nothing new to wear."

   "It's supposed to thunderstorm tomorrow. How will I get to school?"

   "Yum, that chicken smells so good, I can't wait until dinner!"

   Students can base their examples on real conversations and actual experiences. Have students share their real-life conversations and tell what is revealed through each.

7. Students can analyze the dialogue in the narratives found in this book and determine what the dialogue does for the narrative. Discuss.

Punctuating Conversation

Refer to this sheet to help you write grammatically correct dialogue.

1. **Quotation marks go around the exact words that a person says.**

   "Marianne studied every day after school. Can you believe she missed being outdoors the first week of spring for one silly test?" Sarah laughed.

2. **Periods, question marks, exclamation points, and commas go inside quotation marks.**

   "Do you think you did well on the test? You didn't even study one smidge!" Spencer replied.

3. **Commas set off quotations.**

   "Study? What you are looking at," stated Sarah confidently, "is a genius. I memorize information and facts the second I see them."

4. **If a quote is one sentence that is divided, a comma is placed inside the first set of quotation marks, and another comma is used to set off the rest of the sentence.**

   "Sarah," Spencer demanded, "you didn't answer me. Did you do well on the test? I see it hanging out of your notebook. If you are Einstein, prove it!"

5. **When a quote is divided and written as two distinct sentences, begin the second sentence with a capital letter and no comma preceding the second sentence.**

   "I was absent a few days last week, wasn't I?" Sarah reminded Spencer. "I mean, so Marianne got a 100, and all of the bonus questions right, so what? Hasn't the weather been just wonderful? I'm putting away my winter clothes tonight."

6. **When the speaker changes, begin the next quotation with a new paragraph.**

   "The weather will only get nicer, Sarah." Spencer pulled his test from a spiral notebook. "I got an 87."

   "Oh, I love spring. It only happens once a year, you know." Sarah admired the daffodils in the window boxes. "Besides, there is a makeup test next week."

Quoting Reference Material

1. **When quoting material, put quotation marks around the words taken directly from the sources.**

   In her lecture on female singers, Miss Jones stated, "Whitney Houston is the most versatile, accomplished singer on this planet."

2. **If paraphrasing, or conducting research and restating information in your own words, no quotation marks are necessary.**

   According to my music teacher, Miss Jones, Whitney Houston is the greatest female singer in the world.

Chapped Lips

The wind whipped at our faces and numbed our noses, forcing the three of us to run into the closest store. We struggled with the door. Megan pushed, Sarah and I pulled, and somehow we managed to blast through the door.

"Oh!" Megan shouted so that the customers stared, "My face is an iceberg!"

"I'm an icicle!" agreed Sarah's chattering teeth.

I breathed into my fuzzy mittens. "I think my lips are about to fall off."

"Tell me about it," Megan agreed. "Point me to the lip balm."

Megan quickly walked while Sarah and I read the aisle placards.

Sarah pulled a tube from the display. "My dad recommends this brand to his patients."

Megan glanced at the price and muttered, "I wonder how much commission he gets." Then she announced, "I don't have that much money. And I wouldn't waste it on dumb lip stuff anyway." Megan sneered, half-serious, half-joking, at Sarah, who returned the half-playful, half-annoyed look.

I was one-hundred percent serious when I said, "Would you two squabble over something important?" Then Megan and Sarah's half-mean, half-amused sneer turned on me, and we all laughed.

"It's the cold, Desiree, it makes our hearts freeze." Megan held her hand dramatically over her winter coat.

"Yes," Sarah added, "cold-blooded, venomous reptilian snakes are what we've become."

"I don't have much," I ignored their comments and emptied my pockets, "only fifty cents."

"I have about a quarter to add." Megan heard Sarah snort. "What was that for, Miss High and Mighty Privileged One? I do have money, you know, but I didn't know we would get caught in the North Pole on our way to the library!"

Chapped Lips *(cont.)*

"Relax, I was only clearing my throat," Sarah retorted. "I'm getting the good stuff." Sarah pranced away, then turned and added, "and I'm not sharing. My dad says sharing lip balm spreads germs."

"Well, la, dee, da," Megan sang, "so Desiree and I will suffer with more cracks than the sidewalk? What a good friend."

"Sharing lip balm should be no indication of friendship." Sarah aimed the lip balm tube at us.

"Hey, don't point that at me, I haven't said a word," I exclaimed, "and the more you two bicker, the more your lips crack."

"Meg, truce?" Sarah begged, "I'll see if I can get some free samples from my dad. Then you can have the good stuff, too."

"Oh, Miss High and Mighty!" Megan curtsied, "Hail to the Queen."

Sarah rolled her eyes and walked down the aisle toward the register.

"Meg," I tried to put out the fire in her eyes, "it is kind of gross sharing lip stuff. Come on, let's go to the library."

Megan smiled. "We deserve the best, you and me. Remember that."

"So what if Sarah's father is a doctor? She's our friend. Friendship isn't about money. Let's go!" I said.

After we found an empty table at the library and grabbed the current and back issues of our favorite magazines, I felt a tinge of envy when Sarah once again pulled out her lip balm and smoothed layer after layer on her lips. I wanted to say, "Sarah, you've put that on a billion times in less than a half hour," but refrained.

But when Megan pulled two packages of the very same lip balm from her deep coat pocket, I felt like I was walking across a frozen pond, listening to the threatening creaks and cracks warning me not to proceed. I felt myself falling through when Megan handed me my own and Sarah laughed. Their glee drowned me when I saw Megan's red glove high-five Sarah's blue mitten in congratulatory praise. The three of us had always been such close friends.

Chapped Lips *(cont.)*

Discussion Questions

1. Identify the figurative language and discuss how it enhances the narrative. _____

_____

_____

2. What are the conflict(s) and conflict types(s) of "Chapped Lips"? _____

_____

_____

3. Write how you feel in the cold, utilizing all of the five senses. _____

_____

_____

4. Describe the friendship among the three girls. _____

_____

_____

5. Do you know someone who has shoplifted? Write about the circumstance. _____

_____

_____

6. What is the theme of "Chapped Lips"? _____

_____

_____

Writing Activities

1. Freewrite what you would have done in this situation.

2. Write Sarah's point of view as if she were writing a diary entry about her day.

3. Imagine that the surveillance cameras caught Megan shoplifting. Write as if you are the surveillance camera. What did you see?

4. You are the variety store owner, and know Megan's family. What do you do now that you have proof Megan shoplifted?

5. Does Desiree remain friends with Megan and Sarah? Write a dialogue Desiree has about her time at the library with her family during dinner.

6. Write another ending to "Chapped Lips." Give the story a new title, if you would like. Share it with your classmates.

Standards and Benchmarks: 1A, 1B, 1C, 1D, 1E, 1H, 1I, 1J, 1K, 2A, 2B, 2C, 3A, 3B, 3C, 3D, 3E, 3F, 3G, 3H, 3I, 3J, 3K, 3L

Same Story, Different People

Write a narrative using one of the following scenarios or stories, or brainstorm your own real or fictional scenario. Use yourself as one of the characters, but also describe and retell the same event from three other points of view. You may add details to the scenario as desired.

Illustrate the incident, and write the scenario underneath. Add the four different perspectives on index cards around the scenario. Add a picture, photograph, or magazine cutout to the four different perspectives, if possible. Mount the project on poster board and display it in the classroom.

Sleepover Madness

You are at a sleepover. It is midnight. Popcorn is smashed in your sleeping bag, you forgot your pillow, another scary movie has been popped into the VCR, and someone is snoring.

Home Alone

Your parents are going to return from work late. One is at an important, unscheduled meeting, and the other is stuck in traffic. Leftovers have been pulled from the refrigerator. When you sit down to eat, your sibling coughs all over your plate.

Pet Romp

You are in the pet shop watching all of the different animals. Someone is purchasing a canary, another shopper is choosing one of the eight kittens. The dog grooming demonstration has begun, and people surround the pet groomer, who is covered in dog hair.

Spilt Milk

The express line sign at the grocery store reads, "10 items or less," but the fellow in front of you has a cart full of groceries. The checkout person has headphones on and is be-bopping to the music. You are scanning the headlines of *Gossip Magazine* when you drop the gallon of milk, and it sprays all over everyone around you.

Spatial Setting

When you incorporate setting into your narrative, you set the scene for the reader. Now they are able to visualize where all of the events take place. Although you have an image of the setting in your mind, it is important to remember that your reader is unfamiliar with the place; the more details you provide, the more the reader can visualize the setting.

Spatial details assist in the readers' understanding of a setting. Spatial words are clues showing where things are—next to, underneath, behind, in front of, on the other side, covering the windows, on the floor, etc.

Consider this sample setting:

> *She entered the living room. A couch, two chairs, and a fireplace were in the room. Candles were lit, and a picture of flowers hung on the wall.*

All right, so a list of the objects in the room has been provided. You know you are in the living room, and there is a couch, two chairs, a fireplace, etc. But you cannot see the room. What you may picture might be different from what your classmate next to you pictures, and that may also be different from what the author wanted you to see.

See how spatial words help us see the room:

> *She entered what appeared to be the living room. A navy blue couch was against the far wall, and above it was a painting of wildflowers in a gold frame. On the table in front of the couch two white candles glowed. On either side of the couch were two floral print chairs with cushions as fluffy as clouds. Even though the fireplace on the opposite side of the room was not lit, the room looked warm and cozy.*

Spatial Setting *(cont.)*

Revise the following settings to include not only spatial words or phrases but also descriptions that help us see the place. Provide an illustration to accompany your description. You may choose to draw the setting first so you have a clear picture from which to work.

Setting One

He walked into the back room, and there was so much stuff he didn't think he would have time to sort through it all. When he touched a cobweb, he tried to shake it off and knocked over a whole bunch of things.

_____

_____

_____

_____

_____

_____

Setting Two

When the horses stopped, everyone got off and admired the scenery. The horses drank from the stream, and we sat in the meadow to rest. The mountains were big, and the tops were covered with snow.

_____

_____

_____

_____

_____

_____

Same Setting, Two Views

Often the same setting is viewed differently by two people. Each one will notice different details, movements, sounds, and scents within the same place. Here are some exercises to get you writing descriptions of settings from different points of view.

Winter Blizzard

Write two descriptive sentences to contribute to a class "Winter Blizzard" description. The descriptions should not include personal opinions like, "I can't stand the cold," or "I love it when school is canceled!"

Based on the class description of a winter blizzard, choose two characters from below who may view the winter blizzard differently. Complete a character sketch for each of the two characters using the template on page 81, and then write a narrative paragraph of your chosen character's response to the snow using the first person point of view.

- snow skier

- senior citizen

- toddler

- snow plow driver

- highway patrol officer

- ice-cream vendor

Doctor's Office

Using the setting of a pediatrician's office, write about a visit to the doctor using the perspective of two characters from below. Before choosing two characters, cluster the word *doctor* in your writing journal. Share your experiences, both good and bad, with your classmates. Now write two narratives, based on your imagined thoughts for each character. (As an extension, try using personification. What exactly are those aquarium fish thinking about? How about the box of tongue depressors—what are they thinking?)

- mother

- ill child

- healthy child for check-up

- pediatrician

- father

- nurse

Powerful Titles

Titles are essential to narrative writing because a strong title may encourage someone to read your story. Titles hold great power. A title should not reveal too much of the story; rather, a title should pique, or stir, curiosity. After reading a narrative, the reader should understand the significance of the title and how it related to the narrative. If after completing the narrative, the reader is confused by the title, then the reader may feel that he or she missed something. Remember, the title is the first impression the reader has of your story. When creating titles, brainstorm a list of several possibilities, and then choose what you feel is the strongest for your narrative.

Standards and Benchmarks: 1A, 1B, 1C

Summer Vacation

Imagine you were assigned the topic, "Write a story about your summer vacation." As a class, brainstorm titles that would make someone interested in your summer.

Standards and Benchmarks: 1A, 1B, 1C, 1D, 1K

Face Lift

Brainstorm a list of your favorite books in your writing journal. Put a star next to your favorite. As editor-in-chief, you have decided not only to retitle the book, but also to design a new and improved cover for the book. Share your design and new title, explaining their significance to the class.

Standards and Benchmarks: 1A, 1B, 1C, 1D

Autobiography

Brainstorm 10 titles for your autobiography. Choose one that you feel creates the most intrigue. Create a cover for your autobiography and display on a bulletin board.

Standards and Benchmarks: 1A, 1B, 1C, 1D

Superstar

Brainstorm at least ten titles for a biography about your favorite superstar. Create a book cover that would appeal to all types of readers.

Children's Book Titles

Use one or both of the following activities to encourage students to think about book and story titles.

What Can You Tell from a Title?

Compile a list of children's books, writing only the titles on the board. Have students choose the titles of books they are interested in reading, and those that they may reject simply because of the title. Students should volunteer their predictions of the contents of the children's books based on the titles alone.

Have groups of students read selected children's books, analyze the significance of the title, determine whether a more suitable title could have been assigned to the book, and brainstorm a list of title suggestions.

Title, Title, Who Has a Title?

Have students read teacher-selected narratives with the titles omitted. The class should brainstorm a list of titles, giving reasons for their suggestions. After the author's title is revealed, the class will discuss the significance of the title and offer opinions as to the strength of the author's choice. (The narratives in this book can easily be reproduced without their titles and used for this exercise.)

Suggestive Titles

Provide students with the following list of provocative titles and ask them to write a narrative to fit the title. Use the Plot Jot Technique, page 38, to assist in prewriting.

- *The Prince and the Potato*
- *The Life with Nine Cats*
- *The Roadrunner Gets a Flat*
- *He Said Purpose, Not Porpoise*
- *It's the Whistle I Miss*
- *A Diamond, Not a Pearl*
- *The Day the Café Closed*

- *Sardines in My Lunch*
- *Now the Real Work Begins*
- *Hope in a Bottle*
- *That Was Chicken, Right?*
- *Planet Janet, Away!*
- *Frank, the Fire-Breathing Tortoise*
- *Hamsters Ate My Homework*

Standards and Benchmarks: 1A, 1B, 1C, 1D, 1E, 1F, 1J, 2A, 2B, 2C, 3A, 3B, 3C, 3D, 3E, 3F, 3G, 3H, 3I, 3J, 3K, 3L

Titles for the Millennium

Many changes are taking place in the new millennium. You have been elected president of Title Company, Inc., and must assign titles to the following things.

1. New Automobile

Title of Automobile _____

Reason/Symbolism of Title _____

_____

Type of Car_____

Illustration of a New Automobile

2. New Restaurant

Name of Restaurant_____

Type of Food Served _____

Location _____

Sample Menu_____

3. New Flower

Title of New Flower _____

Significance of Flower _____

_____

Illustration of a New Flower

4. New Planet

Name of Planet _____

Significance of Name_____

_____

Illustration of a New Planet

5. New State

Name of State _____

Location _____

What State Is Known for _____

Compile all six titles into a "Millennium Titles" booklet, which also needs an appropriate title! Each page should include a minimum of three reasons for the new title, all information specific to each object, and an illustration. Use your word processor to design an attractive page layout.

Three Scoops Please!

You are creating three new ice cream flavors, and must assign titles to each of these new flavors. Add a description to each new flavor using adjectives, sensory imagery, and figurative language. Illustrate your triple scoop ice cream cone to accurately depict your three new flavors.

Flavor #1:_____

Description: _____

_____

_____

_____

_____

_____

Flavor #2:_____

Description: _____

_____

_____

_____

_____

_____

Flavor #3:_____

Description: _____

_____

_____

_____

_____

_____

May I Help You?

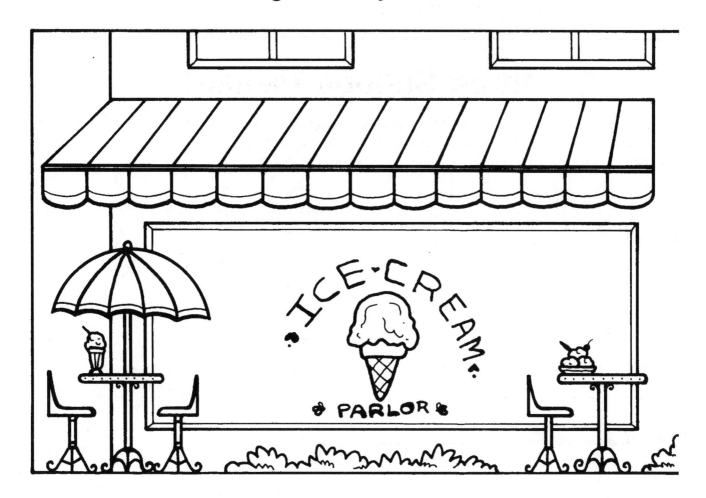

Not many people come to the ice-cream store to get vanilla. In fact, as long as I've worked here, I've never scooped a plain old vanilla ice cream cone. Today, though, was different. The customer who just left ordered vanilla, even after I asked, "Sir, have you tried our flavor of the month?" He hadn't, and he insisted on vanilla. "We have many other flavors, sir." Vanilla, though, suited him fine. It isn't that I have anything against vanilla. It's just that vanilla was so ordinary.

"Half-gallon, please. Vanilla." The customer held out a crisp twenty-dollar bill.

"Vanilla." I was dumbfounded. "Vanilla?" I grabbed a half-gallon container and began scooping. All the while, the other thirty-one flavors cried for my attention. "Sir, if you want a half-gallon of vanilla, plain old vanilla, don't you think you could go to a grocery store? I mean, vanilla is vanilla." And, I dropped my voice to a whisper to make the gentleman feel like I was revealing a secret, "you'll be paying almost triple the price here."

May I Help You? *(cont.)*

"No, dear. Vanilla is not vanilla." He smiled. "Ice-cream parlor vanilla is quite different." He leaned on the counter and continued. "Every Saturday, when I was a child much younger than you, I would go to the ice-cream parlor and, with one nickel, buy a scoop of vanilla. Pretty soon, I needed a dime."

"Inflation?" I asked.

The man laughed. "No, Roseanne, who eventually became my wife."

I was just about done scooping the clumps of vanilla ice cream into the half-gallon container.

"Now I hope this vanilla ice cream will trigger her memory. Make her remember me . . . or herself . . ." He handed me his money. "Ah, who's kidding who? Every now and then, us old folks like a dish of good ice cream!"

I gave him his change and his ice cream, and when I heard the chime of the door close, I grabbed a spoon and scooped out a chunk of vanilla. Plain old vanilla. Deliciously perfect.

May I Help You? *(cont.)*

Activities

1. What is the significance of the title? Brainstorm other possible titles and share your suggestions with the class.

2. Why does the salesclerk feel "vanilla is vanilla"? Do you agree with this statement? Discuss the literal and figurative meanings of this phrase.

3. What is the theme of the narrative?

4. What is the conflict and type of conflict?

5. Using the Rainbow Comparison Graphic Organizer (page 83), compare store-bought and ice-cream shop ice cream. You may actually want to have a class "taste test."

6. Using one of your invented flavors from "Three Scoops, Please!" pretend that you are an employee at the ice-cream shop and are trying to sell your flavor of the month to your next customer.

7. The man in the narrative takes the vanilla ice cream to his wife, Roseanne. Write a narrative experimenting with point of view. Share with the class.

8. Write a similar story, but use a unique ice-cream flavor such as marshmallow nut or honey pear. How does this change the characters? setting? plot? Change the title to suit your new story and share it with your classmates.

9. Use your computer's draw or other art program to create an ice-cream shop in which you would like to work. Write a narrative description based on your drawing.

10. Complete the following similes and metaphors:

    a. The chocolate ice cream was _____.

    b. The strawberry ice cream tasted like _____.

    c. The cone was as crunchy as _____.

    d. The scent of the ice-cream shop was _____.

    e. All the ice-cream choices were _____.

Writing a Fable

A *fable* is a short narrative—usually no more than two pages in length—that teaches a lesson. This lesson is often stated through a moral at the end of the fable. Characters in fables are generally animals that take on human traits or inanimate objects such as rocks and rivers that are personified as real, live people. There are not more than three characters in most fables.

As a class, brainstorm a list of fables. Working in groups, assign several fables to each group. Each group should summarize each fable using the 5W+H questions, and state the fable's moral.

Each group should also list the human characteristics and traits of the characters in the fable on a chart such as the one below labeled "Vices and Virtues." *Vices* are a character's bad traits, and *virtues* are a character's good traits. Here is an example of an animal's vices and virtues:

Peacock

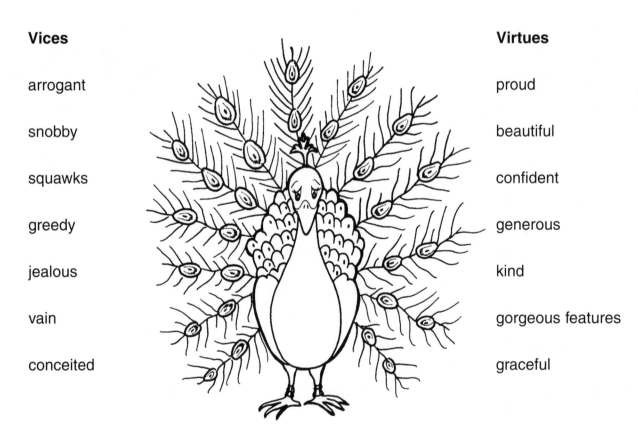

Vices	Virtues
arrogant	proud
snobby	beautiful
squawks	confident
greedy	generous
jealous	kind
vain	gorgeous features
conceited	graceful

Read "The Seagull and the Crab" beginning on page 105 and complete the activities that follow it. Then, write an original fable, using the Fable Template on page 108.

The Seagull and the Crab

It was a glorious day at the beach. Crab skittered across the sand, only to bump into Seagull, who was preening his feathers.

"Hey, watch where you are going." Seagull flapped his wings angrily. "Why are you in such a hurry?"

"The sandcastle building contest is in two days, and I am looking for a nice spot to practice." Crab clicked his claws. "This looks like a great spot! Not too many shells and no seaweed."

Quickly, Crab constructed a mountain of sand and moved away to admire his crafty creation.

"That is one giant blob!" cawed Seagull. "It looks nothing like a sandcastle!"

Crab danced around his enormous pile of sand, his castanets clackety-clacking.

Seagull hopped across the sand and scratched his webbed feet in the sand like a batter preparing to hit a grand slam. "I am a flier. I have visited the great castles of the courtyards, perched on drawbridges, and even scooped fish from moats. The sandcastle contest prize will be mine!" Seagull let out a screech so loud, Crab hid behind his giant sand hill. Seagull's beak carved and pecked the sand.

"Oh my, oh my!" Crab yawned and stretched his claws. "You are finally finished, feathered friend! It is beautiful. You are a great architect! Those peaks and turrets, the gates and bridges, the exquisite details! A fine designer, to be sure, to be sure!"

The Seagull and the Crab *(cont.)*

Suddenly, a wave chomped at the shoreline. Seagull rocketed upward, and Crab anchored himself to the sand.

When the foamy froth retreated, Seagull's sandcastle was completely crushed. Crab's blob stood tall and proud.

Seagull and Crab sat on the sand and cried.

"I'll never win the sandcastle contest!" they both bawled simultaneously. Seagull sighed, "You are a fine builder, Crab. Your mound of sand, although not a castle, defeated the ocean. An incredible feat."

"And you . . . and you . . ." twittered Crab, "you built the finest castle I have seen! Design my home by the sea, and I will build it!"

Seagull cocked his head and barked orders at Crab, who obeyed every one. Crab's claws were hammers and chainsaws—they flung sand, drilled holes, and crafted Seagull's masterpiece. Crab's blob was transformed into a castle rivaling Poseidon's.

"Wave, ho!" shouted Seagull. A ferocious wave pounded the sand. Crab hid in his castle's dungeon, and Seagull positioned himself on the castle turret. The wave inhaled the shore, but the castle was unharmed.

"Together, we will win the contest!" exclaimed Seagull.

"To be sure, to be sure!" sang Crab. "Together, we will conquer all!"

The Seagull and the Crab *(cont.)*

Activities

1. Brainstorm lists of vices and virtues for Seagull and Crab.

2. Illustrate the fable. Share the illustrations.

3. Brainstorm a list of titles for the fable.

4. Identify the moral or morals of "The Seagull and the Crab."

5. Brainstorm other situations Crab and Seagull could be in that would reflect other morals. Use 5W+H questions to create a plot outline. In groups, write another fable using Crab and Seagull. (You may wish to use the the Fable Template on page 108.) Share the fables with the class.

Writing Activities

1. Write a paragraph responding to the question, "If you were an animal, what would you be and why?" As a prewriting exercise, brainstorm a list of virtues and vices for your chosen animal. Students should use the Rainbow Comparison Graphic Organizer on page 83 to sort out the similarities and differences.

2. Read several fables and select a favorite. Analyze the fable, and then write a modern fable paralleling the original fable. For example, turn "The Tortoise and the Hare" into a story about a snowboarding race. The characters should be human and the settings real. Illustrate the fable and share it with the class.

3. For a major writing project, brainstorm a list of at least 30 animals. Choose four animals from this list and brainstorm what makes each animal interesting, including facts and physical characteristics. Then, complete a vice and virtue chart on each of the four animals. Next, choose two animals to be the main characters in an original fable, using the Fable Template (page 108) as a guide. For your final presentation, revise and illustrate your original fable, act out the fable with a partner for the class, or use *KidPix*™ to animate the fable and show it to the class.

Fable Template

Use this template to prewrite an original fable or to think about and discuss one that has already been written.

Title of fable: _____

Who: _____

What: _____

Where: _____

When: _____

Why: _____

How: _____

Moral: _____

Characters	Vices	Virtues
1. _____	_____	_____
	_____	_____
	_____	_____
	_____	_____
	_____	_____
2. _____	_____	_____
	_____	_____
	_____	_____
	_____	_____
3. _____	_____	_____
	_____	_____
	_____	_____
	_____	_____
	_____	_____

Conflict: _____

Type of conflict: _____

How the conflict was resolved: _____

Tall Tales

Read the following facts about tall tales.

☆ Tall tales originated in North America when settlers relied on these narratives to help them believe in the "American dream."

☆ The American dream was that everyone could achieve prosperity, overcome obstacles, be independent, rely on themselves, and keep their identity in the New World.

☆ Tall tales are based on fictional characters who used intelligence, ingenuity, and their own resources to survive the difficulties confronted in the New World, to explore and expand the West, and to break free from England.

☆ The characters in tall tales have unique abilities, skills, and physical or personality traits enabling them to perform amazing feats.

☆ Tall tales are based on hyperbole—the reader knows that the narrative is not true, but it still provides hope, inspiration, and courage. Tall tales show the reader that anything is possible, and we have to find and utilize our abilities to confront our conflicts.

☆ Tall tales are humorous.

☆ The characters in tall tales often do not realize the purposes of their special features or of unique talents; rather, these characters "stumble" upon them.

☆ Tall tales contain all the narrative elements—characters, setting, plot, conflict, and theme.

Activity

Read or listen to several tall tales. Identify the elements that make each story a tall tale. Then work in small groups, selecting one of the following periods of history to brainstorm as a prewriting exercise for creating your own tall tales.

- hardships confronting the first settlers
- conflicts created in trying to gain independence from England
- difficulties faced in expanding westward
- conflicts during the Civil War

After brainstorming, write a tall tale. Illustrate the tall tale. (You may wish to use *KidPix*™ to animate your tall tale instead.) Create a bulletin board so that everyone can read each other's tall tales.

Standards and Benchmarks: 1A, 1B, 1C, 1D, 1E, 1H, 1I, 1J, 1K, 1L, 2A, 2B, 2C, 3A, 3B, 3C, 3D, 3E, 3F, 3G, 3H, 3I, 3J, 3K, 3L

Tickets, Please!

Today is Valentine's Day, and for the first time there were two gifts waiting for me on the kitchen counter. The handwriting on the pink envelope was my mother's, and on the red envelope, my father's. Instead of being happy, though, my heart ached.

I remembered a conversation I had with my parents a few weeks ago. I didn't regret what I said, but I did regret how I had said it. I had just returned from a friend's birthday party where I watched her unwrap gifts from her friends and family. Her father had picked something out especially for her; even her mother didn't know what it was.

For me, this was unusual. My mother did all of the special occasion shopping. My dad had no idea what was in the packages. All he did was sign his name to the card, or my mother did it for him: "Love, Mom and Dad." Now, I knew my father loved me. I never doubted that. But I did wonder why he didn't mind that my mom did all of the special occasion shopping.

"Dad, why do you just sign your name to our cards and never pick out something for us yourself?" I demanded when I returned home.

Neither he nor mother understood what I meant. When I clarified my question, he didn't say a word. He left the room.

My mother cast her disapproving shadow across the room and stated, "I'm disappointed in you. We're a family. How could you hurt your father like that?"

Tickets, Please! *(cont.)*

I hurt him? He hurt me! At every special occasion he would wink, crack his knuckles, and say, "It's a surprise—I hope you like it!" In truth, my dad was just as excited for us to open our packages because their contents were a surprise to him as well, even if he was supposed to be the giver.

It may sound like a silly problem, but when I saw my friend open up her present just from her father, I wanted that moment. I wanted my father to want that moment. The episode was never brought up again, until today, Valentine's day, the next special occasion.

My mother's card to me was beautiful, as always. Words like "treasure" and "forever" and "love" were underlined. I knew she had poured over every card in the stationery store and selected this one just for me. In the envelope were two movie passes—one for her and one for me. There was a sticky note on one that read, "We'll decide on a movie together." Mother was so thoughtful.

As always, I expected my Dad's card to be corny, one of those "ha-ha" cards, not a keepsake card that I'd hide in my special memory box. But it wasn't. On the front was a picture of a carousel with ponies painted in primary colors and suspended from gold columns. There were no lacy hearts on it, though. I sensed my father had really looked for this card, because it didn't seem like a regular Valentine card.

When I opened it, I knew I was right. There was no machine-scribed message inside, just my father's words in his own hand. I imagined him scribbling it before taking off for the office, but, again, I was wrong. My eyes misted as I read his message:

When you were little, we'd ride on the carousel. You probably don't remember, but I do. I'd stand beside the horse, bobbing up and down, around and around, traveling a great distance, yet going nowhere. I'd hold you, my eyes glued to your face. Your eyes believed the horse was real, and your smile convinced even me that the blue pony with the white mane and yellow eyes could travel to the end of the rainbow. You wanted to stay on the carousel forever, and I wanted to freeze our moment together. It was a time when you needed me to get you to the saddle and then to return you safely to the ground. I doubt you want to ride on the carousel anymore, I'd probably get dizzy in my old age(!), but I want you to know I'm always beside you, whether you believe it or not, and I love you.

Dad

Tickets, Please! *(cont.)*

Wrapped in tissue paper without a bow was a small tin of lemon drops, the kind covered in powdered sugar. I smiled. They were my dad's favorite, but he used to share them with me. My mom and I always got him a tin until a few years ago, when the candy store in town closed. I wondered where he got them. I placed a lemon drop on my tongue and closed my eyes, desperately trying to remember the rides on the carousel with my father.

Taking a plastic bag from a drawer, I filled it with the remaining lemon drops and placed them under my father's pillow. Then I put the tin in my memory box, along with my father's Valentine's Day card. When I pulled the box out from under my bed, it tipped and a gray ticket stub fluttered out. When I held it between my thumb and forefinger, I remembered. I remembered the tinny music, the grasp of my five fingers around my father's hand, the ponies that brought children to their destination, though they never left the circle. I remembered holding so tightly to the ticket, afraid it would fall through the wooden planks and I'd miss my ride to my special place.

I smiled. I knew my father would never have let that happen—not in the past, and not in the present or future.

Tickets, Please! *(cont.)*

Discussion Questions

1. Identify and describe the conflict in "Tickets, Please!" _____

   _____

2. Discuss the effectiveness of the title. Brainstorm alternate titles. Which one would you choose? Why? _____

   _____

3. Highlight the sensory imagery that you find in the story. What does the character see, smell, taste, touch, and hear? _____

   _____

4. Characterize the father. How would you describe him? What vices and virtues does he possess? _____

   _____

5. Identify the possible themes of "Tickets, Please!" _____

   _____

Writing Activities

1. Write a continuation of "Tickets, Please!" from the point of view of the father when he finds the lemon drops under his pillow.

2. If you have a treasure box, a scrapbook, or a special place where you keep things you want to keep, what are you saving in it and why?

3. Design a Valentine's Day card. The recipient of the card should be your mother, father, or guardian. The text of the card should be a minimum of five lines. Write a message that you think the recipient will like.

4. Write a letter to your mother, father, or guardian, letting this person know how important he or she is. The letter should be a narrative, describing one or more memories you have shared with this person. Place the letter under this person's pillow. Share the reactions with your class. Write in your journal how doing this act made you feel.

5. Write a narrative about a time you were rude to a parent or older relative. Remember, in nearly all narratives, the conflict is resolved.

Interviewing

Interviewing is an excellent way to gather information. Through a successful interview, the author can get information directly from the source. The best interviewer will have knowledge of the person or situation, so that time is not wasted asking unnecessary questions. Interviewing is similar to the work of an archaeologist. The better prepared the archaeologist is—choosing a location to dig, knowing what he or she is looking for, knowing about the facts about the time period, preparing the site, having tools on-hand—the more successful the archaeological dig.

Conducting interviews can be exciting, too. Secrets, valuable information, and outstanding stories can be discovered during an interview.

So, dig and unearth some good information!

Interviewing Guidelines

1. **Schedule an appointment.**

   Set the time, date, and place for the interview.

   Confirm the appointment the day before.

   Make sure a parent or guardian can attend the interview session.

   Allow at least 30 minutes to one hour for the interview.

2. **Research thoroughly.**

   Use the 5W+H technique for assessing the purpose of the interview.

   Brainstorm a list of what you know about this person and his or her situation, and brainstorm a list of what you would like to know.

3. **Formulate interview questions.**

   Arrange the interview questions sequentially.

   Questions should be open-ended (see page 115).

4. **Create a good first impression.**

   Dress appropriately.

   Use your best manners.

5. **Ask questions one at a time.**

   Write down the answers carefully.

   Ask the interviewee to repeat, if necessary.

   Ask other questions if they arise.

6. **End the interview courteously.**

   Thank the person for assisting you.

   Ask if you can phone or e-mail if other questions arise.

   Send a final copy of your narrative to the interviewee as a thank you.

Writing Open-Ended Questions

The questions below are poorly written because the response to them can be a simple "yes," "no," or other one-word answer. Revise the questions so that they are open-ended. An open-ended question makes the interviewee think about his or her response and expand upon it. Interviews also go better when the person being interviewed knows that you are well-prepared.

Share and discuss your open-ended questions with the class. As a class, determine which questions may or may not be good ones to ask during an interview.

1. Where did you grow up? _____

_____

2. Where did you go to school? _____

_____

3. Are you pleased with your career choice?_____

_____

4. Do you have a large family? _____

_____

5. Do you have any hobbies? _____

_____

6. Is your job challenging? _____

_____

7. Did you have any pets growing up/now? _____

_____

8. Where is your favorite place to go? _____

_____

9. What is one goal you have? _____

_____

Interviewing Activities

Use the following activities to get students involved in interviewing people and then composing their interview material as a narrative.

Peer Interview

Practice interviewing classmates. Remind students to first brainstorm what they know about the classmate and to determine what they would like to know about their peer. An interview question list should be formulated and the interview conducted. Remind students that they are incorporating the information into a narrative, which means the interview must also be a story with conflict, theme, characters, setting, and plot, instead of a catalog of facts.

Class Interview

Conduct a class interview. The teacher should arrange for a local business person, town official, or school official or administrator to be interviewed by the class. Again, the class should be well prepared before the interview is conducted. After the interview, students should complete individual summaries using the 5W+H techniques. Each student will write a narrative of the interview; additional research may be necessary.

Television Interview

Students should watch television interviews by respected interviewers to learn from their techniques. Discuss. Students should complete the 5W+H to summarize the interview. Students should brainstorm a list of questions they would like to ask if they could conduct a follow-up interview. Questions should be revised to be open-ended and should be listed sequentially. Share.

Radio Interview

Students should listen to taped radio interviews by respected interviewers to learn from their techniques. Students should compare radio and television interviews and the different skills involved in each using the Rainbow Comparison Graphic Organizer on page 83. Students should complete the 5W+H to summarize the interview and then brainstorm a list of questions they would ask in a follow-up interview. Questions should be open-ended and arranged sequentially. Share.

Family Interview

Students will interview a family member about the past. Students should first complete a character sketch of this person to help determine their interview questions. Students should also brainstorm what they know, and what they'd like to know about this relative. After the interview, students should organize the narrative and complete the narrative template.

Using Technology

All of the interview projects can be taped, and presented either as a radio or a television interview. The students can also create a *PowerPoint*™ presentation based on the interview, or a web page about the individual interviewed.

Gathering Information

Why should you gather information about the person whom you are interviewing?

You will be more knowledgeable.

Your writing will be more accurate.

You will feel more confident when writing your narrative.

Your readers will see that you put effort into your topic.

There are other ways to gather information about a person or topic besides an interview. Some of these ways follow:

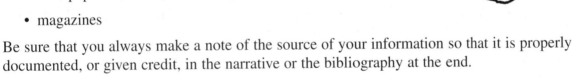

- go directly to the source
- from prior knowledge
- books
- encyclopedias
- Internet Web sites
- friends
- relatives
- parents
- television programs
- newspapers
- magazines

Be sure that you always make a note of the source of your information so that it is properly documented, or given credit, in the narrative or the bibliography at the end.

Common Bibliography Format

Book: Author. <u>Title</u>. City: Publisher, date.

Magazine: Author. "Article Title." <u>Magazine</u>, date of magazine, pages of article.

Encyclopedia: "Heading of Entry." <u>Name of encyclopedia</u>. Volume #, date written out in words, page numbers.

On-line source: Author of site. "Title of Web Site" [on-line], (date of visit), Internet address, pages of Web site utilized.

Television: "Title of Program." Date and time of program, channel.

Interview: Name of interviewee. Date, time, and place of interview.

Newspaper: Author. "Title of article." <u>Newspaper</u>, date of newspaper, pages of article.

Note: Dates should be written out in words, not in numerals.

School librarians and computer/media specialists can assist in the demonstration of techniques for gathering information. Use their talents and knowledge for showing students how to use specific equipment and resources.

Self-Revision Checklist

Step 1

Read your story aloud. Pause at the commas and stop at the periods. If you find yourself pausing where there is no comma, you may be missing one that needs to be added. If you find yourself needing to stop where there is no period, check to see if you have a run-on sentence or simply a sentence that is too long. Often your ear can hear mistakes that your eyes miss. Maybe you have left out a word, or something doesn't seem quite right. Instead of stopping the flow of revising the narrative as you are making corrections, put an X in the margin. After you finish reading, go back and add the corrections where X marks the spots.

Step 2

List the parts of the story for proper sequencing of events.

Beginning:_____

Middle: _____

Climax: _____

End:_____

Step 3

Check to see that all components of a successful narrative are included.

Conflict: What is the conflict? How is the conflict resolved? Is the conflict presented in the beginning so the reader is intrigued?

Characters: Are the characters original or stereotypes? Can you identify or visualize the characters? Are the characters' traits and personalities consistent with their actions?

Setting: Can you imagine where the narrative takes place?

Flow or pace: Are there unnecessary scenes? Scenes that need to be added?

Dialogue: Does the dialogue contribute to the story? Is the dialogue realistic?

Step 4

Read the narrative for description. Identify five examples of figurative language, sensory imagery, and strong verbs.

Step 5

Revise: Give the narrative to a small group for reader-response suggestions (see page 119).

Use reader-response comments for completing your revision.

Step 6

Produce the final narrative.

Step 7

Publish the narrative by sharing it with the class in an oral or written format.

Reader Response

It is important for readers to be honest, but considerate, with their opinions. Readers also need to make their responses specific, so that the author is clear about what his or her readers liked and did not like about a piece of writing.

Read the following vague or weak comments below that are followed by examples of more specific comments. Discuss why the specific comments are an improvement over the vague ones.

I liked it.

I liked it because it was so descriptive that I got lost in the story.

It was too long.

I thought the scene in which the characters were taking a walk could be taken out.

The beginning was boring.

The beginning needs to have dialogue.

What's the theme?

I found the message confusing. Was it about honesty or pride?

The conflict wasn't resolved.

The ending would be stronger if the characters talked to each other.

The title was dumb.

The title is weak. It needs to be about the theme.

The main character was cool.

I liked the main character because of his great clothes.

Steps in Reviewing Narratives

Step 1: Identify any problems with the author's narrative.

Be specific with your comments. Use examples from the story to share what you mean.

Step 2: Consider the author's feelings.

A statement such as, "This is the worst story I have ever read!" is cruel and does not help either you or the author.

Step 3: Speak for yourself.

Give your view only! "I enjoyed reading your narrative because a friend of mine just lost her dog, and now I can better understand how she feels."

Step 4: Identify the good.

Be specific about what you like. "When you described the roller coaster ride, I got dizzy!"

Step 5: Share your final reactions.

"Overall, I thought the aliens forgave their captors too quickly. The captors were so mean. But the ending had a neat twist. I'd like to read a sequel!"

Proofreader's Marks

Using the following proofreader's marks is important when completing a self- or peer-revision because everyone uses the same symbols. It is easy for the author to understand what he or she needs to fix because the author and the reviewer use the same editing marks.

Editor's Mark	Meaning	Example
ℓ	Delete	It was ~~was~~ very tiny.
≡	Capitalize	the boy ran quickly.
/	Use lowercase	Many Athletes ran in the marathon.
∧	Add a word	I want an ice ^cream^ sundae.
RO	Run-on sentence	Who's there ^RO^ what do you want?
frag.	Sentence fragment	Although the peddler's cart. ^frag.^
SP	Spelling error	Monkies^SP^ swung in the trees.
∽	Reverse letters or words	Five books on were the shelf.
⊙	Add a period	Children played all day⊙
∧ (comma)	Add a comma	I like apples‸peaches, and pears.
∨	Add an apostrophe	John˅s puppy is cute.
⌄⌄ ⌄⌄	Add quotation marks	˅˅Help! ˅˅cried.
¶	Begin a new paragraph	"Hello," said Carla.¶ "Hi," Beth replied.
#	Make a space	I love French#fries.
⌣	Close the space	He lives in the country ⌣ side.
stet	Do not delete (Let it stand.)	The ^stet^ ~~beautiful~~ swan flew away.

Standards and Benchmarks: 1A, 1B, 1C, 1D, 1E, 1H, 1I, 1J, 1K, 2A, 2B, 2C, 3A, 3B, 3C, 3D, 3E, 3F, 3G, 3H, 3I, 3J, 3K, 3L

My Cove

"Me next! Me next!" Garrett, Elizabeth's older brother cried.

"Okay," Father said, "and what is your special place?"

"The cove." Garrett sighed, as did Father, Mother, and Sophie. I sighed, too. The cove was only a memory now.

"I remember hiking through the sea-grass trails and meeting the ocean," reminisced Garrett.

"Oh, and the picnics, remember our picnics?" breathed Sophie. "Momma, you packed the basket with ham and cheese sandwiches, delicious! Those chocolate-chunk cookies that were wrapped in foil so they wouldn't get crushed. The stale bread we fed to the sea gulls that swooped like fighter pilots. Never mind ants—those seas gulls are scavengers! Remember when they stole the sandwich right out of my hand?"

"Yes, I do remember that!" I laughed. "And I remember waving to the captains of the sailboats! The beautiful colors of the sails getting smaller and smaller as they chased the horizon."

Waves of laughter filled the room. The noise rose and subsided like the changing tide.

"Monica," reminded Sophie, "you were only a baby; you couldn't possible remember."

"I do remember!" I exclaimed. "I went to the cove countless times. Remember when my sandal broke and Father carried me?"

"That was me," Sophie clarified.

"You weren't even walking when we moved here, Monica-Shmonica," Garrett teased.

My Cove *(cont.)*

"Sorry, Lamb. Your brother and sister are correct. You only saw the beauty of our cove once, cradled in my arms. Actually, I think you slept the entire time, lulled by the gentle ocean's surf."

"You remember our stories," Father explained, "and how wonderful it is that you have a brother and sister who have shared these stories with you so you feel like you know the cove."

Garrett and Sophie understood Father's you-better-be-nice tone and politely excused themselves from the room.

I left the room, too, but journeyed to the backyard and found a shady spot under my dogwood tree. I rested against the familiar bark, inhaled the forest's perfume, and looked upward at the green leaves floating on their blue canvas. The pink flower petals scattered across the grass, and I felt their smoothness, the same feeling as the inside of a shell. Shells I remembered holding at the cove.

I was there, and I remember. A place like the cove cannot be erased or forgotten. Shutting my eyes, I held my shell, placed it against my ear, and listened to the soothing ocean sounds. Sharp sea grass tried to block my passage through the trails, furry soft plumes displayed their splintery stalks. The trails divided, but I followed the salty smell beckoning me. The ocean greeted me by washing ashore its treasures—rounded pieces of frosted sea glass, blue, green, brown, and translucent. Barnacles clung to driftwood, seaweed searched for its queen—me! I wrapped the cool strands around my head and draped necklaces across my shoulders.

I saw the flocks of sea gulls playing, fighting, swooping, and soaring, homing in on crabs or schools of shiners. I remembered the lazy clouds, sunning themselves on their blue towel. I remembered thanking them for creating a sun block, even for an instant. I remembered splashing in the gentle tide pools and wading in the shallow water.

Mother said I was there but once. My heart was there a thousand times more.

My Cove *(cont.)*

Discussion Questions

1. Does Monica truly remember the cove? _____

   _____

   _____

2. Identify the conflict in this narrative. _____

   _____

   _____

3. Is the conflict resolved? _____

   _____

   _____

4. Find examples of sensory imagery and figurative language and discuss how they enhance the narrative. _____

   _____

   _____

5. Identify the theme of "My Cove." _____

   _____

   _____

Writing Activity

Brainstorm a list of places that you remember from childhood. Select one place that brings back special memories and use this place as the topic for a cluster.

Next, write a narrative about this special place, describing the setting so vividly the reader believes that he or she has been there too, just as Monica feels she has been to the cove.

Finally, create a collage of images depicting this place and the memories it evoked. The narrative and collage can be presented to the class.

Standards and Benchmarks: 1A, 1B, 1C, 1D, 1E, 1H, 1I, 1J, 1K, 2A, 2B, 2C, 3A, 3B, 3C, 3D, 3E, 3F, 3G, 3H, 3I, 3J, 3K, 3L

The Looth Tooth

On the bus ride home from school, I couldn't help eavesdropping. Two kids in front of me had megaphones for mouths and were so excited you would think it was the last day of school. The excitement was only over a loose tooth one of them had. Call me crazy, but maybe I'm maturing, like my mother says. I think I can blame the deodorant my mother left on my bureau a few weeks ago when she told me that maturing boys need the stuff. I thought those primary school kids were silly—hooting and hollering like they got a good prize in a box of Cracker Jacks™.

I leaned forward and stared at the kids (older boys are allowed to stare at kids on the bus for no reason), and they didn't even shrink. They didn't even acknowledge my superiority! The one kid with hair the color of carrot juice was wiggling a tooth the size of a mini-marshmallow. It dangled there from from his upper gum, and it would have hypnotized me if I had stared any longer at it, watching it sway back and forth, back and forth.

The other kid's squeaky voice, which sounded like new sneakers on tile, snapped me back to reality when he spoke. "Yikes, cripes, elephant stripes! That's a doozer, all right. The tooth fairy will bring you a whopper for that piece of ivory, for sure!"

The Looth Tooth *(cont.)*

"Tooth fairy?" I murmured to the foam oozing out of the tear in the pine-needle green seat in front of me. "Tooth fairy."

I turned faster than I ever had in a game of Red Light, Green Light. "You believe in the tooth fairy?" When a fellow as mature as me, one who smells like his dad in his armpits, speaks to primary grade kids, they answer, believe me.

Neither boy said a word. They looked at me with marble eyes and bed-head hair, peanut butter and grape jelly crusted in the corners of their mouths.

"What, do you have potatoes in your ears?" I demanded. "I said, 'Do you believe in the tooth fairy?'"

"Golly, do we," Freckle Boy breathed.

"Have you ever seen her?" The other boy asked. He hoisted himself up on the back of my seat so I could see the saliva on his tongue. He had gaping holes in his mouth where teeth used to be. Both top and bottom gums bulged. White daggers poked through the swollen red flesh. I cringed. "Look at Kenny's tooth. Isn't it a doozer? The tooth fairy will bring him a whopper for sure!"

"Hey," Kenny drew himself close to me. I could see my reflection in his eyes and smell his peanut butter breath. "You've got all your big chompers. What was the best thing the tooth fairy ever brought you?"

"That was a long time ago." I huffed. I almost revealed that I wore deodorant.

"What do you think the tooth fairy will bring Kenny?" Gum Boy questioned. Kenny leaned closer and opened his mouth so wide I could see sandwich crusts wrestling with the cherry pie and potato chips in the pit of his stomach. I couldn't keep my eyes off that tooth flailing around like a person on the end of a bungee cord.

The Looth Tooth *(cont.)*

"Get that thing away from me!" I yelled.

The boys giggled and fell backward against their seat. "Isn't it a doozer?" Gum Boy repeated. "The tooth fairy has never seen anything like that, I bet!"

"I'm staying up all night," Kenny stated.

"Then you'll see your mom or dad all groggy-eyed in a bathrobe sneakin' in and leaving a quarter under your pillow." I felt like I had eaten too many hard-boiled eggs. The sight of Kenny's tongue wiggling and jiggling around in the hole where the tooth fell from, though still clinging to the vein like a monkey swinging on a vine, made me feel crummy.

The boys stared at me. How come I felt like I was guilty of taking a bite out of each chocolate in the box and then putting it back?

Fortunately, around the corner was my bus stop. I hopped out of my seat and made a note to never sit in the back of the bus again. The path to the front was at least a mile long. I felt all sweaty and wondered if the deodorant was working.

I couldn't eat the after-school snack my mom made for me. All I could see was Kenny and Gum Boy looking at me like I had stolen their Halloween candy.

I thought about how I had awaited the arrival of the tooth fairy and wished I could have stayed awake to actually see her.

Kenny's tooth was a whopper, for sure. I bet he'd get a pack of trading cards, or a magnifying glass, or maybe even a couple of crisp, new dollar bills. Then again, perhaps he wouldn't wrap his tooth in a tissue and put it smack dab under his pillow. Maybe tonight his mother would leave deodorant on his bureau.

The Looth Tooth *(cont.)*

Discussion Questions

1. Identify the types of conflict and how they were resolved in "The Looth Tooth." _____
   _____

2. Discuss the effectiveness of the title. Brainstorm other titles. Choose one. Explain your choice. _____
   _____

3. Is the narrator mature? Why do you think so? _____
   _____

4. Why does the narrator reveal the truth about the tooth fairy? _____
   _____

5. How does the narrator feel after revealing the truth?_____
   _____

6. Discuss the characterizations of Kenny and Gum Boy. _____
   _____

7. Locate examples of figurative language and sensory imagery. Discuss them in class.
   _____

Writing Activities

1. In your journal, freewrite about the tooth fairy.

2. Draw a picture of your imagined tooth fairy.

3. Have students complete the 5W+H about a time they had a loose tooth and then lost it.

4. With your class, brainstorm on the board a list of people, places, or things that you believed in as a child but no longer do, for whatever reason. Share your reasons for your disbelief.

5. Write a personal narrative about a time you discovered something that you thought was true or real and it turned out to be not true or real.

Standards and Benchmarks: 1A, 1B, 1C, 1D, 1E, 1H, 1I, 1J, 1K, 2A, 2B, 2C, 3A, 3B, 3C, 3D, 3E, 3F, 3G, 3H, 3I, 3J, 3K, 3L

Hitting the Hay

Everyone was excited about the sleepover except for me, yet I couldn't think of any excuse for staying just for the party and leaving before we hit the hay. The guys would call me a baby, and I'd never be able to show up at school again. So, I rolled up my navy and red sleeping bag, popped my toothbrush into my knapsack, along with an extra T-shirt and boxer shorts, and wondered how I'd survive the night.

Usually at night, I fall asleep to the hum of the dishwasher or the quiet drone of the late-night news. How could I fall asleep without a good-night kiss from my mother? I zipped up my knapsack. How could I not go to the sleepover? Both were impossible.

Little did I know that the word "sleepover" did not mean sleep. Sleepover meant popcorn, popcorn fights, movie after movie (ignoring the "Be Kind, Rewind" plea), wrestling, name calling, an occasional "Go to sleep!" shout from the invisible parent, bad jokes, burping contests, and asphyxiating smells that filled our sleeping bags. Sleepover meant conversations about sports, girls, sports, girls. Sleepover meant cookie crumbs, soda, video games, and more wrestling. A sleepover is not brushing your teeth, not changing your shirt or your underwear, not caring about what you look like or smell like, and definitely not sleeping.

Sleepovers are definitely fun. And sleepovers are tiring. Returning home, I fell into my bed. My pillow had missed me and welcomed me back. Home. I felt my blanket tuck itself around my shoulders, and felt my mother kiss my cheek.

"Nice to have you home," she whispered in my ear.

"It's wonderful to be..."

Hitting the Hay *(cont.)*

Discussion Questions

1. Identify the conflict in "Hitting the Hay." _____

    _____

    _____

2. What is the theme? _____

    _____

    _____

3. Discuss the significance of the last line of the narrative. _____

    _____

    _____

Writing Activities

1. Students should cluster the words *sleepover* and *home*.

2. Students should brainstorm a list of fears they have. They may share stories of childhood fears that have been overcome, or fears they have now. Share "sleepover" stories.

3. Students should freewrite how they feel about sleepovers. What do they like about sleepovers. What do they miss from home?

4. Students should write a narrative about a fear they had or a fear they have. Students should include the reason for this fear and how they deal or dealt with it.

Standards and Benchmarks: 1A, 1B, 1C, 1D, 1E, 1H, 1I, 1J, 1K, 2A, 2B, 2C, 3A, 3B, 3C, 3D, 3E, 3F, 3G, 3H, 3I, 3J, 3K, 3L, 4A, 4B, 4C, 4D, 4E, 4F, 4G

Place Setting

In my family, Christmas Eve is more important than Christmas. We are Polish, and we follow Polish traditions. Actually, it is my grandmother, Babcia, who herds us outside for one of our first traditions. For the first time tonight, she leaves the kitchen, and we follow her into the quiet night.

We must see a star before we eat. All we see is a flicker—only an airplane. Our laughter fills the night. The first twinkle, high in the east, makes us smile. Vigilea, the vigil, waiting for Christmas, has begun.

We march inside, single file, to the table decorated in white. Candlesticks and a vase of holly nestle on hay which resembles the manger and reminds us of the humble, quiet birth. An extra place is set for the visitor who will join us in spirit at midnight. Before the food is served, the thin wafer we call oplatek (oh-pwa-teck) is passed from generation to generation. The wafer is shared as wishes of good health and happiness bond us.

Bowls of borscht (beet soup) are ladled into small china dishes. The magenta color is beautiful, and when a dollop of sour cream swirls through the steam on a silver spoon, the soup cools and thickens. Babka—light, flaky bread—is even more delicious with butter, and the stewed prunes and apricots sweeten the crusts of bread. Platters of fish and potato pancakes are emptied quickly, but Babcia's oven produces an endless supply to feed her family.

Chrushchiki (crew-shtick-ee)—fried pastry with powdered sugar and a hint of cinnamon,—disappears faster than the presents are opened on Christmas Day. Kolendy (ko-lahd-nee), or songs, are sung around Babcia's piano. Babcia remains in the kitchen, clearing and washing. She enjoys listening to our harmonious voices, and knowing we are happy makes her happy.

When Babcia died, I realized how important Christmas Eve was. The first year, we all did something different. We had no shepherd to lead our flock. But this year, we have come together. I set two extra places at the dinner table. One is to remember Babcia.

Place Setting *(cont.)*

Discussion Questions

1. What is the conflict? When is the conflict introduced? How is the conflict resolved?

   _____

2. Characterize Babcia. _____

   _____

3. What is the theme of "Place Setting"? _____

   _____

4. What is the significance of the title?_____

   _____

5. The language is simple and direct. Why? _____

   _____

6. Identify the sensory imagery and discuss how it enhances the narrative._____

   _____

7. Is the narrator sad about Babcia's death? Explain. _____

   _____

8. The author uses a technique called "defining within context." This means that the author defines unfamiliar terms so the reader does not have to stop to look for a glossary or reach for a dictionary. Identify the instances within the narrative that the author defines terms or ideas within the story. Discuss the technique. _____

   _____

Writing Activities

1. Cluster the word *tradition* in your writing notebook.

2. Create a brainstorm about your family traditions.

3. Write a narrative about a family tradition that occurs in your culture or religion. All unfamiliar terms should be defined within the context of the narrative. Bring in a dish, illustration, map, or costume reflective of your heritage to share with other students.

4 Use the Internet to research the country or countries from which your ancestors came to the United States. Write a brief narrative describing some of the traditions of that country or countries.

Standards and Benchmarks: 1A, 1B, 1C, 1D, 1E, 1H, 1J, 2A, 2B, 2C, 3A, 3B, 3C, 3D, 3E, 3F, 3G, 3H, 3I, 3J, 3K, 3L

Creature Creation

You will write a fictional narrative about an imaginary creature, using this template for prewriting. You may choose to draw the creature first.

Name of the creature _____

Scientific name of the creature_____

Circumstances of discovery _____

    Who _____

    What _____

    Where _____

    When _____

    Why _____

    How _____

Creature's purpose _____

Life span _____

Appetite _____

Special powers _____

Habitat _____

Personality _____

Color _____

Skin Texture _____

Physical Description:

    The head of a _____

    The tail of a _____

    The body of a _____

Write a Plot Jot for your story about the creature here. _____

Questions about plot jot _____

Characters for the story _____

Conflict of the story _____

Theme of the story _____

Out of This World

For this fictional narrative assignment, you will create a new planet in our solar system and write a narrative about this planet.

Use the template below as a prewriting guide.

Name of planet _____   Illustration of planet

Reason for name _____

Planet's shape and size_____

Position in the solar system_____

Climate_____

Topography _____

Atmosphere _____

Life forms _____

Vegetation_____

Circumstances of discovery

    Who_____

    What _____

    Where _____

    When_____

    Why _____

    How _____

Write a Plot Jot about your story about the creature here. _____

_____

_____

_____

Questions about plot jot _____

Characters for the story _____

Conflict of the story _____

Theme of the story _____

Standards and Benchmarks: 1A, 1B, 1C, 1D, 1E, 1H, 2A, 2B, 2C, 3A, 3B, 3C, 3D, 3E, 3F, 3G, 3H, 3I, 3J, 3K, 3L, 4A, 4B, 4C, 4D, 4E, 4F, 4G

Sports Trading Card

Use this template to create a nonfiction narrative about a sports figure.

Name of figure _____

Sport and team_____

Position _____

Height _____ Weight _____ Age _____

Date of birth and hometown _____

Career highlights _____

_____

Statistics _____

Strengths _____

_____

Education _____

Training _____

Why did this athlete become interested in this sport? _____

_____

Conflicts overcome _____

_____

Future goals and/or ambition _____

_____

_____

_____

_____

Interesting facts_____

_____

Illustrate the sports figure here:

Put on a Pedestal

Use this page and the template on page 136 to help you write a nonfiction narrative about someone whom you admire.

1. Cluster the topic *role model*.

2. Brainstorm traits that a role model has. Discuss them with your classmates.

3. Brainstorm role models in various categories:

Teachers _____

_____

Politicians _____

_____

Historical figures_____

_____

Writers _____

_____

Religious figures_____

_____

Helping professionals (doctors, nurses, etc.) _____

_____

Coaches _____

_____

Family members _____

_____

4. Use the "Put on a Pedestal" template to assist you in researching the role model of your choice. Your final presentation should include a computer generated presentation.

Then have an "Awards Day" on which you and your classmates will read your narratives as if you are presenting awards to your role models.

Put on a Pedestal Template

Complete the following questionnaire about your role model:

Name _____

Age _____ Occupation _____

Write four adjectives to describe this person. _____

1. How did your role model get to his or her present position?

   _____

   _____

2. How do you know your role model? When did you first think of this person as a role model?

   _____

   _____

3. Write down some triumphs and accomplishments or hurdles that your role model overcame.

   _____

   _____

   _____

   _____

4. What have you learned from your role model?

   _____

   _____

   _____

   _____

5. What do you want others to know about your role model?

   _____

   _____

   _____

   _____

6. If you could give your role model one thing, what would it be and why?

   _____

   _____

7. If your role model could give you one thing, what would you want it to be and why?

   _____

   _____

A Helping Hand

Write a personal narrative about a time you lent a helping hand below to someone. What were the circumstances? Who did you help? Use the graphic organizer below to assist you in writing a narrative.

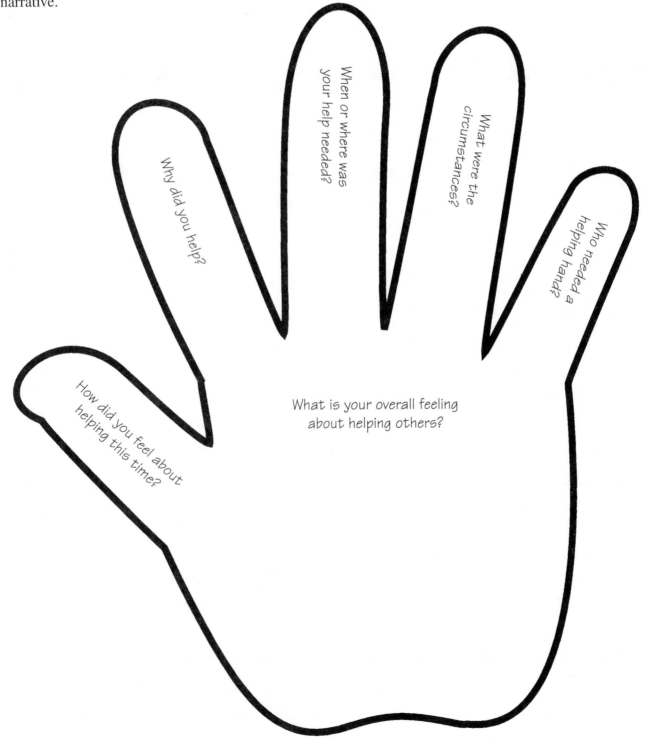

Creating a Coat of Arms

Use the template below for brainstorming about yourself, writing your thoughts in the areas provided. You can also create a coat of arms from a character's point of view to aid in characterization or to think up other narrative topics.

People I love	What angers me	What I fear
What I do with friends	What brings me joy	What I worry about

My talents/hobbies	My role model

My special places

Narratives About Literature

When students read novels, short stories, or children's books, it is important to validate the reading experience not only through book reports but also through critical thinking and creative writing. The following narrative writing activities allow students the opportunity to immerse themselves in the text, make them view it in a new perspective, and gain a better understanding of the narrative elements. All narrative assignments follow the writing process and should contain all of the narrative elements.

Favorite Spot

Students should imagine that the main character has taken him or her to the main character's favorite spot, which should be from a scene in the narrative. First, students should describe the place. Then the students can tell what was revealed or seen there. What do the students think about this place? What was the purpose in viewing this place?

My Special Place

Students take one character from the narrative to their own special place. Bringing the character there should have a purpose. Does it help the character deal with the conflict? Does it give them hope? Students can describe this special place and give reasons for taking the character there.

That's Not What I Would Have Done!

Students should take the perspective of the main character and write what they would have done if in a similar situation. Students should recount a similar personal experience to justify their actions. Students should compare and contrast their experience with that of the character's experience.

Scrapbook

Students should create a scrapbook about the main character. After brainstorming items found or kept in a scrapbook, students will create a scrapbook containing a minimum of fifteen mementos. Students should accompany the scrapbook with a narrative explaining why these fifteen mementos were preserved in their scrapbooks.

Dialogue to Narration

Students will take a dialogue excerpt from a narrative and rewrite it using narration only. Students should compare the two scenes and determine why the author chose to write the scene using dialogue.

Narration to Dialogue

Students should take a narrative excerpt and rewrite the excerpt using dialogue. Students should analyze how the narrative changes with dialogue and determine why the author chose to write the scene as straight narration, rather than with dialogue.

Narratives About Literature *(cont.)*

Prequel

Students can write a narrative *prequel* to the narrative. A prequel is about what happened before the narrative begins.

Sequel

Students can write a narrative *sequel* to the narrative. A sequel is the continuation of the story.

Diary Entry

Students can write a diary entry from a main character's point of view during the climax, or turning-point, of the narrative.

Changed Actions

Students can change the actions of a minor character, thus altering the plot. Students can experiment with point of view.

Manipulating Conflict

Students can change the conflict confronting a main character. The new conflict must fit the plot sequence, although the ending may change.

Three Conclusions

Students will summarize the beginning and middle of a narrative, and then offer three different versions of the ending. All endings must be unique but plausible.

Award Ceremony

Students can present an imaginary award to one of the characters. What is the award, and why is this character the recipient? Students can first write an introductory speech, and then an acceptance speech from the character's point of view.

Celebration

Students can add a celebratory scene to the narrative. The scene must be an integral part of the narrative.

Personal Assessment Rubric

The rubric is weighted at 100%. Ten is the highest score for each item. Add up the 10 numbers to get total score.

1. All prewriting activities are completed.

   10   9   8   7   6   5   4   3   2   1   0

2. During the revision process, the narrative shows not only revision but also the addition of reader-response comments.

   10   9   8   7   6   5   4   3   2   1   0

3. The theme is clear without being directly stated.

   10   9   8   7   6   5   4   3   2   1   0

4. The first paragraph or part of the narrative is interesting and draws in the reader; the conflict is presented right away.

   10   9   8   7   6   5   4   3   2   1   0

5. The characters are lively, realistic, and described well.

   10   9   8   7   6   5   4   3   2   1   0

6. The setting is clear and described so it can be visualized.

   10   9   8   7   6   5   4   3   2   1   0

7. All parts of the story (beginning, middle, climax, and end) follow in order. The conflict is resolved.

   10   9   8   7   6   5   4   3   2   1   0

8. Figurative language, sensory imagery, and strong action verbs contribute to the story.

   10   9   8   7   6   5   4   3   2   1   0

9. Spelling and punctuation are correct.

   10   9   8   7   6   5   4   3   2   1   0

10. The narrative is published according to directions.

   10   9   8   7   6   5   4   3   2   1   0

Nonfiction Narrative Assessment Rubric

The rubric is weighted at 100%. Ten is the highest score for each item. Add up the 10 numbers to get total score.

1. All prewriting activities are completed thoroughly and thoughtfully.

   10   9   8   7   6   5   4   3   2   1   0

2. Research is gathered from a variety of sources, and the bibliography is properly formatted.

   10   9   8   7   6   5   4   3   2   1   0

3. The narrative tells a story, complete with conflict, characters, setting, and theme.

   10   9   8   7   6   5   4   3   2   1   0

4. The narrative has a beginning, middle, climax, and end, and follows sequentially.

   10   9   8   7   6   5   4   3   2   1   0

5. Research is correctly documented within the narrative.

   10   9   8   7   6   5   4   3   2   1   0

6. Figurative language, sensory imagery, and strong action verbs contribute to narrative.

   10   9   8   7   6   5   4   3   2   1   0

7. Spelling and punctuation are accurate.

   10   9   8   7   6   5   4   3   2   1   0

8. The revision process shows attention and insight.

   10   9   8   7   6   5   4   3   2   1   0

9. The final presentation follows the guidelines.

   10   9   8   7   6   5   4   3   2   1   0

10. The interview is conducted appropriately. Preparation is evident.

   10   9   8   7   6   5   4   3   2   1   0

Fiction Narrative Assessment Rubric

The rubric is weighted at 100%. Ten is the highest score. Add up the 10 numbers to get total score.

1. All prewriting activities are completed thoroughly and thoughtfully.

   10   9   8   7   6   5   4   3   2   1   0

2. All elements for particular narratives are included.

   10   9   8   7   6   5   4   3   2   1   0

3. Characters are realistic and described well.

   10   9   8   7   6   5   4   3   2   1   0

4. The setting contributes to the story.

   10   9   8   7   6   5   4   3   2   1   0

5. Figurative language, sensory imagery, and strong word choice draw the reader into the narrative.

   10   9   8   7   6   5   4   3   2   1   0

6. Conflict is introduced in the beginning and resolved logically.

   10   9   8   7   6   5   4   3   2   1   0

7. The narrative is original, properly sequenced, and has smooth transitions that link the beginning, middle, climax, and end.

   10   9   8   7   6   5   4   3   2   1   0

8. The short story shows evidence of revision.

   10   9   8   7   6   5   4   3   2   1   0

9. The spelling and punctuation are correct.

   10   9   8   7   6   5   4   3   2   1   0

10. The final presentation is neat, organized, and follows specific requirements.

    10   9   8   7   6   5   4   3   2   1   0

Narratives About Literature Assessment Rubric

The rubric is weighted at 100%. Ten is highest score for each item. Add up numbers to get total score.

1. All prewriting activities are completed.

   10   9   8   7   6   5   4   3   2   1   0

2. The narrative shows understanding about the actual literature on which the narrative was based.

   10   9   8   7   6   5   4   3   2   1   0

3. The narrative shows evidence of revision and incorporation of reader-response comments.

   10   9   8   7   6   5   4   3   2   1   0

4. The characters are described accurately, and stay in character with the original narrative.

   10   9   8   7   6   5   4   3   2   1   0

5. The parts of the story (beginning, middle, climax, and end) follow sequentially.

   10   9   8   7   6   5   4   3   2   1   0

6. Figurative language, sensory imagery, and strong action verbs contribute to the story.

   10   9   8   7   6   5   4   3   2   1   0

7. The spelling is correct.

   10   9   8   7   6   5   4   3   2   1   0

8. The punctuation is accurate.

   10   9   8   7   6   5   4   3   2   1   0

9. The narrative is creative, unique, interesting, and adds a new dimension to actual literature.

   10   9   8   7   6   5   4   3   2   1   0

10. The overall presentation meets guidelines.

   10   9   8   7   6   5   4   3   2   1   0